John McDowell Leavitt

New World Tragedies from Old World Life

With Other Poems

John McDowell Leavitt

New World Tragedies from Old World Life
With Other Poems

ISBN/EAN: 9783744665940

Printed in Europe, USA, Canada, Australia, Japan

Cover: Foto ©Thomas Meinert / pixelio.de

More available books at **www.hansebooks.com**

NEW WORLD TRAGEDIES
FROM OLD WORLD
LIFE.

NEW WORLD TRAGEDIES
FROM OLD WORLD LIFE;

WITH OTHER POEMS.

BY JOHN M. LEAVITT.

NEW YORK:
HARPER BROTHERS,
FRANKLIN SQUARE.

LONDON:
SAMPSON LOW, MARSTON, SEARLE, and RIVINGTON,
CROWN BUILDINGS, FLEET STREET.

1876.

(*All Rights Reserved.*)

Entered according to Act of Congress, in the year 1876, by the Author, in the Office of the Librarian of Congress at Washington.

CHISWICK PRESS: PRINTED BY WHITTINGHAM AND WILKINS,
TOOKS COURT, CHANCERY LANE, LONDON.

TO

BITHIA!

CONTENTS.

	Page
AFRANIUS	1
Ariston	61
The Jewish Captives	139
Faith	199
The Roman Martyrs	217
The Deluge	237
The Periods	255

VARIOUS PIECES:—

Our Flag	275
Old England	276
Shadows	277
The Photograph	278
Liberty	281
Our Country	282
Leaves	283
The Hills	284
Paul Parson	287
Asel's Soliloquy	290
A Song in Heaven to Home	292
A Parlour Prologue	293
Near my Birth-place	295
Israel's March-word	295
The Heart's Master	296
For the Book of a Friend	298
The All-Maker	299

CONTENTS.

Various Pieces (*continued*):—

	Page
Invocation	300
The Rainbow	301
A Vision of Solyma	302
The Useful and the Beautiful	309
Written for a Lady, to be given with her Photograph	310
On a Birthday	311
Life	312
The Deity	313
Solicitude	314
Regret	315
Abraham Lincoln	317
Birds at Morn	318
Above	318
The Clouds	320
Boabdil's Lament on the Hill of Tears	323
Ayxa's Rebuke for Boabdil's Lament	325
Madrigal	327
Serenade	328
Art and Nature	328
My Rose	330
The Real and the Ideal	331

AFRANIUS.

AFRANIUS.

ACT I.

Scene I.—*Rome.   Palace of the Gothic King.*

KING.

OLD Sibyl, I am glad to see thy face,
Whose every feature of my Zala speaks,
And tells the love that breathes to her I love;
She more a Roman seems, and these her skies,
Than of my blood, and born 'mid Gothic snows.
How fares my child?

SIBYL.

O King, in person, well.

KING.

Why then this wildness in thine eye and tone—
This look that I have seen in summer skies,
Which, dubious, show a smile, and drop a tear
While thunders gather in some viewless cloud?

The teacher of my child should shed round joy,
And brighten like a morning of young Spring.

SIBYL.

A captive Roman seam'd by age and care
Has little heart for laughter, or for love.
Can the scathed oak, at will, burst into bloom,
And garland its old limbs with fresh young leaves?
Can ice gush into streams when suns are hid?
The Alps are rock, yet on the mountain's heart
One flower moves tears, as its blue eye looks up,
And pleads with Heaven to keep the tempest back.

KING.

Thy words show peril to my daughter near;
Speak out thine heart!

SIBYL.

    With this once threaten'd tongue?

KING.

Dwell not on that, old nurse, when anger flash'd.
Sweeping each mem'ry on its tide of fire
Of service to my child, from life's first bud
Till womanhood in her glows like a rose.

SIBYL.

But why should I to thee a fault unfold
That will upon a Roman bring down stripes?

KING.

Because—refuse, and I thy lips will force,
And from them wring the secret of thy soul.

SIBYL.

Thy hand a sceptre sways, but sways not me.
Touch'd by the flame that burn'd in Rome's old days,
Thy wither'd slave thine empire here defies.

KING.

Stay, Sibyl, stay! nor like the sorceress stare,
Who on our Gothic hills Rome's conquest sang!

SIBYL.

My love for Zala forces me to tell
What Rome's own kings from me could not compel.
'Tis some time since I saw how Julius sigh'd,
And gazed on her sweet face, and watch'd her
  form—

KING.

But why not this before?

SIBYL.

     Thy rage, O King,
Restrain, and hear me through! A short hour since,
By frenzy urged, when glow'd the noontide heat,
Nor stirr'd a breeze to cool the burning cheek,
Julius, at Zala's feet, avow'd his love,
While she, astonish'd, spurn'd the slave away.

KING.

And now she asks my vengeance on his head.
Ho! Julius! Julius! slaves, bring Julius here!

SIBYL.

Nay! with the eloquence of tears she pleads

That I his crime should not disclose to thee;
But fearing his wild flame I disobey.

KING.

What! will she ask the brazen'd villain's life?
Who 'neath our yoke dares such a suit must die.

Enter Servants *with* JULIUS.

Viper! thy shining skin did tempt this hand
To warm thee and be stung—base spider thou,
Spinning sly toils to snare my Zala's heart!

JULIUS.

Hear me, O King!

KING.

Mean villain, say no more!
And didst thou, slave, address my daughter's ear,
And importune her with the gaze of love?
Strip him, and let the rod beat out his life!

JULIUS.

Oh, spare my flesh the scourge! I pray thee spare!

KING.

When first our Goths possess'd these towers of Rome
Thy pensive face and eye my fancy won,
And waked a wish to cultivate thy gifts.
Before thy mind Rome's learning was unroll'd;
Thy skilful hand soon touch'd the lute's sweet
strings;
Thy magic voice stirr'd depths of melody,

And I, near mine own Zala, placed thee then
As a companion more e'en than a slave;
Yet thou didst dare to whisper thy vile vows.
Lay hold, and scourge him till his breath be gone!

Enter ZALA.

ZALA.

Oh, father, spare! I do beseech thee, spare!

KING.

These Roman dogs our silly kindness spoils.
The coming feast which marks that glorious hour
When our brave Goths first scaled these walls of Rome
Shall bind with heavier chains the bloated knaves.

ZALA.

Oh! must poor Julius die! is here no hope—
No door where Pity may an entrance find,
And soften down stern Justice into tears?
His murd'ress I will ever brand myself,
And in the midnight toss, and tear my couch,
Staring to see his pale, reproachful face,
While through my ear will pierce eternal shrieks
Till I will never know the dew of sleep.

KING.

Thy tears prevail. Julius, I grant thy life.
Yet shall thine ear cut off teach with thy blood,
And thy foul loss, its lesson to our slaves.

JULIUS.

O King, I pray thee let me rather die!
Beat, stab, or burn; stain with my gushing blood
The lion's jaws; sink me with hissing snakes
Lone in the sea; in silent dungeons chain
Me to the corpse whose loathsome touch is death,
But clip me, not to live a thing of scorn!

KING.

Julius, enough! thou wilt not change me more.
                                        [*To the attendants.*
Just when the dial points the hour of four,
And ere the shadow of its finger pass
One hair-width from the mark, apply the knife!

SCENE II.—*The Pantheon.* SIBYL *alone.*

SIBYL.

IMMORTAL gods who cradled infant
    Rome,
    Then made the world her throne, oh, are
        ye dead?
Majestic Jove, why sleeps thy thunderbolt
When wretches hurl thine image to the dust?
While Juno was dragg'd down to earth by boys,
Mock'd on our streets, where thy fierce lightnings
    then?

Thy shrines are robb'd, thine oracles are dumb,
Thy children kneel and cry to emptiness.
Mail'd Mars, who, flashing, led Rome's eagles on,
His helmet saw torn from his godlike brow
And to vile uses turn'd, yet stood mute marble.
Yea! she whose Gorgon locks shook hosts with
 fear,
Felt, unavenged, the hammer of a slave.
Thou, crown'd Apollo, image of the sun
Whose glories beam'd in features most divine,
Majestic form, the god of light reveal'd,
Yet shatter'd down by those who hate thy shrines!
Diana's bow, her quiver, and her zone
Ground into dust, and wide o'er Tiber strewn!
Sweet Venus, dream of love, we saw thy head
First batter'd off, then turn'd to ribald jest!
Fawns, Dryads, Nymphs, ye bright divinities
Who smiled o'er earth the wingèd watch of Heav'n,
Your pedestals are void, your statues marr'd;
Shrines, altars gone, and this domed Pantheon bare
Before a murder'd Jew they style their god!
Ye deities of Rome, come back! come back!
Our gold shall pile, our blood shall smear your
 shrines,
And we will lift each image from the dust,
And temples crowd with your true worshippers!

Scene III.—*A walk in the Royal Gardens in Rome.*

QUEEN.

My little Goth, my pretty northern flower
Set in Italia's soil to grow more bright,
Thy father's wife, I am thy mother too.

ZALA.

O Queen, in love I hence will hold thee such,
And e'en as her who gave to me my life.

QUEEN (*placing a rose on* ZALA'S *breast*).

This rose, more than a bud, nor quite a flower,
Which wants one morn to bring its glories forth,
Now thee becomes more than in rounded bloom.
As thou, beyond the girl, nor woman yet,
Wouldst look most sweet on some strong manly
breast.

ZALA.

The Queen doth love her little rose so well
She'd cut its stem and send its beauty off.

QUEEN.

Nay! plant her flower but in a richer soil:
Princes do beg to have its scented bloom.

ZALA.

Her rose she'd sell, its charms would turn to gold,

Take for it slaves, or lands, maybe a crown;
Its virgin blushes change for so much pelf!
Forgive its sorrow for its dang'rous worth.
    QUEEN.
What lovers sigh to wear our beauteous flower—
The brightest in the gardens of the world!
It must not fade and die in loneliness.
Maxentius first would win it to his breast;
His noble form will weigh less than his gold.
    ZALA.
A mountain bear! thy rose in his vast paws!
His beard would prick its leaves, nor would he lose
One precious hair could he a goddess wed.
    QUEEN.
Take Marco then with all his fine estates
And slaves to fill the Capitol.
    ZALA.
      Marco!
A fox whose cunning made him rich—his eye,
His chin, his nose the prowler's race betray—
Sly in his love, his very kiss a trick;
His arms about my waist would make me creep,
And cry—Marco in that warm clasp what plot?
    QUEEN.
Then Caius choose, in Roman houses rich—
In gems, in robes, in steeds, in pictured halls,
High in his birth—if small, most exquisite.

ZALA.

He would my lap-dog make—spoil'd pretty thing,
And with himself well pleased—I'd curl his hair,
His whisker twist, and call him my bright lad,
While he would laugh, the charming mannikin!

QUEEN.

Ah! Jovian then!

ZALA.

A ponderous, splendid ox,
Well fed and strong, whose soul has turn'd to flesh

QUEEN.

Girl, jest no more! The king would have his throne
Stand firm in Rome, and marry thee for this.

ZALA.

The daughter sold, confirms the father's crown—
Bargain'd her heart through craft for policy!
The girl rebels, stands on her womanhood,
And tells the king she chooses for herself—
Ties her own heart to him who calls her wife,
And will a husband wed, but not the state.

QUEEN.

This Sibyl's art! I pray thee, Zala, pause!
Thy parents, not thyself, should plan thy good.
Princes and nobles crowd here for thy hand.

ZALA.

Thou dost say true—my *hand*, but not my *heart*.
Yet blame not Sibyl where mine own's the act.

QUEEN.

Thy fancy weaves, maybe around some slave,
A spell of girlish love—a spangled snare
That dances in the sun to be thy death.

ZALA.

My heart but wants a *man*—a *man* will have—
Nor more, nor less,—'tis Heav'n my fate decrees.

Enter KING.

QUEEN.

O King, thy daughter spurns her father's plans,
And vows that she must wed at her own will.

[ZALA *falls on her knees in tears.*

KING.

My daughter, at my feet lie not to weep
Like some lone rose bent down by night's chill
    dews,
But stand up in the sun, our royal flower,
Thy sweetness shedding o'er our house and life;
So wed that Goth and Roman thee will bless;
Nor for thee earn a father's blasting hate
If thou refuse to prop his tott'ring state!

Scene IV.—*A retired street in Rome.*

LUCIUS.

HAIL my old friend! How sober is thy face!

VARRO.

My mood suits my gray hairs! but thou art fresh
As this young morning air, bright as the sunshine.

LUCIUS.

Yea! I have heard what brings me back my youth,
And makes each burning pulse throb with new joy.

TITANIUS.

To Lucius, Varro, I have told our scheme;
When first he heard he turn'd his face to heaven,
Then clasp'd my hand until the flesh is black;
This aching palm shows still his love for Rome.

VARRO.

His clutch more tight yet round the tyrant's throat,
To leave behind a mark as dark as death!
'Tis *men* we want, to go where Battle bares
His blood-red arm, and on to glory leads.
Not such be ours who test the crowd by straws,
Blown on vile breath where Fortune gilded smiles;
But those for Rome who'll fight and peril all
Where Power enthroned on wrong would drain their blood,

And kindle round their brows the martyr's flame.
Such was our Brutus when he Cæsar struck
Whose grandeur spann'd the world, and touch'd
    the heav'ns,—
A tyrant rending with avenging steel
Made first by Justice keen. Like Brutus yet
May our Afranius stab!

LUCIUS.

              A man of dreams,
Who sighs where he should strike, and weakly
    weeps
Where he should spill but blood—not words but
    blows
Will break Rome's chains, and yet he draws no
    sword.

VARRO.

But in him lurks a soul of fire that stirr'd
By war to flame will scathe this Gothic herd.

TITANIUS.

Nay! at the font the hero's spark was quench'd;
The sprinkling priest has turn'd him to a girl;
Before those drops, sat valour on his helm,
Beam'd from his eye, tower'd in his manly form,
Outflashing from the circles of his sword
Till he 'mid battle's earthquake moved like Mars
When thundering on the gods, and shaking
    heav'n.

LUCIUS.

Yes! lean as love beneath the moon he steals
To sit in tears upon some shatter'd shaft,
Resting his silent head upon his hand
To watch the stars, and gaze on vacancy.

VARRO.

Ye both mistake—the hero's fire will blaze;
A crisis comes—these silken lords of Rome
Who live in homes fond fathers built for them,
Spend gold they never earn'd, and cringe to Goths;
Burning with lust where they should flame with
    hate;
Nought in themselves, who boast their robes and
    slaves,
Dote on the steeds that whirl them to the goal,
Or vaunt the wretch who wins them crowns with
    blood,—
Wantons, whom music lulls in curtain'd beds—
Who have the shapes of men, and souls of boys,
And shake to feel the breath e'en of the spring,
These may by valour win, what cowardice lost,
And learn from stripes in dying manhood's gasp.
But, angry, Julius comes! I'll help his rage.

Enter JULIUS.

Tell me, O slave, thy master how this morn!

JULIUS.

Master, thou fool! A Roman knows no master!

LUCIUS.

Save when the lash shall mark his back with blood,
And his all-quivering flesh proclaim the slave.

JULIUS.

'Twas for the king ye ask'd—then curse the king,
And having done begin and curse again,
Till curses, hot as hate, shall pierce him through.

VARRO.

Oh, bravo, Julius—tell us whence this wrath!

TITANIUS.

The royal tongue has scored for some slight fault,
Or Zala, peevish, order'd him to stripes
Which to a hero turn'd her writhing slave.

JULIUS.

Your jeers I do deserve, since I, a slave,
Content to live for those who pamper'd me,
Have show'd these Goths, more hungry than their wolves,
Our delicate delights whose organs drink
The glorious light of these Italian skies.
But that has happen'd which strikes off my chain;
Henceforth I live to blast the tyrant's life.

ALL.

Farewell, brave Julius, till thy temper cools.

[*Exeunt.*

JULIUS.

I seem hideous—of my proportion shorn;

Each stream will mirror my deformity;
The rounded moon each month will tell my loss;
The sun's full orb will speak it through each day.
I'll feel unfit to dwell 'mid curious beasts;
Ashamed to look my fellow in the eyes;
Doom'd till my death to hear the scoffs of boys,
The suppress'd titter of each giddy girl;
Clipp'd like some dumb beast to bear abroad
The mark and badge of him whose slave I am.
O ear, that thrill'd once with a mother's voice,
Thy savage sev'rance turns my love to hate,
My conscience kills, wakes hell that cries for blood.
Thou, through whose veins Rome's noblest currents
    flow'd,
Dragg'd from thy halls down to a Goth's vile breast,
Smile from thy skies, and hear thine injured son!
Since there I knelt where Jove his image lifts
Majestic as a god, and burn'd to him
The grain whose smoke roll'd o'er the Capitol,
My breast, an ocean, has whirl'd round in fire.
An angel bars the starry gates of light!
Apostate from my faith, I read my doom—
Revenge my heaven! Revenge at last my hell!

ACT II.

Scene I.—*A retired place in Rome.*

AFRANIUS.

Y friends, ye do mistake!

FIRST GOTH.

Afranius, nay!
We well have weigh'd thy power to gain our suit.

AFRANIUS.

'Tis scarce a month I boast these arms mine own;
Nor has the fetter's scar yet left my flesh.
So late a slave I'll hurt you more than help.

SECOND GOTH.

Thy valour moved the king to set thee free,
And gratitude will open thee his heart.

FIRST GOTH.

Behind the throne one moves the royal hand;
Her smile who broke thy chain will aid our cause.

AFRANIUS.

That hint would blast me in her father's eyes,
And hurl me back again to harder bonds.

SECOND GOTH.

'Twas Sibyl whisper'd that the girl was pleased;
Again we pray thee help us in our suit.

AFRANIUS.

Calm Prudence tells me I should shun the risk,
Yet I will dare all peril for my friends.

BOTH GOTHS.

Thanks, Afranius, thanks! long life and thanks!
[*Exeunt.*

AFRANIUS.

Most wretched he who lives on smiles of kings!
O Liberty, thy music midnight storms,
Thy robes the snow, thy bed the mountain's breast,
Thy roof the clouds, thy food the peasant's crust,
I love thy hills yet more than royal halls
Where I do cringe in glitt'ring misery.
Should it be known we at the fountain met,
Beneath the moon, to seal eternal vows,
The eyes of night our starry witnesses,
My Zala's life would flow out in her blood,
While I chain'd low beneath the Tiber's wave
Could strike from Rome no bond! Around is night!
Yet Heav'n has form'd us as the sun and moon,
Which both must shine to bring out earth's best
    bloom.
Wild tempests shake my breast and cloud my life!
Religion, Love, and Rome are struggling here!

Enter JULIUS.

Ha! Julius, how art thou?

JULIUS.

       Afranius, ill!

AFRANIUS.

Our country's shadows will fall on the heart.
Why look'st thou so pale?

JULIUS.

      Thou, Afranius, thou,
Basking in smiles while Romans groan in chains,
Thou, glittering thus, art steel'd to our mean griefs.

AFRANIUS.

Julius, this does me wrong. When flatter'd I,
When bent a pliant knee, when play'd the knave
To gain my freedom and the Goth's good will?
Have I not blush'd for every Roman's shame?
Have I not burn'd for every Roman's wrong?

JULIUS.

Afranius, 'tis most true.

AFRANIUS.

      Why then affirm
That I on Fortune's honours plume myself,
And shut my heart to pity and to grief?
Be blind these eyes when they refuse a tear!

JULIUS.

Weep not, but strike! change sighs to manly
  blows!

AFRANIUS.

Julius, this mystery cease! explain thy words!

JULIUS.

I will!

  [*He pulls aside the hair which is always worn
   long to conceal his loss.*

AFRANIUS.

  O sight most foul and horrible!
Say, whence this blood, this sad disfigurement?

JULIUS.

I loved and on my knees avow'd my love.

AFRANIUS.

Loved! Julius, whom?

JULIUS.

   Zala!

AFRANIUS.

    Zala! Zala!

JULIUS.

Ah! why should anger crimson on thy cheek
As if the girl had vow'd her heart to thee?

AFRANIUS.

And how did she thy suit receive?

JULIUS.

    Receive!
She treated it with sheer, contemptuous scorn,
Deeming it too presumptuous for belief,
While Sibyl told the king, who maim'd me thus.

AFRANIUS.

I pity thee!

JULIUS.

   Pity not me, but Rome !
My griefs are nought while pangs tear her dear
  breast ;
Each statue of her gods hurl'd from its base ;
Her palaces and temples spoil'd by fire,
Or given o'er for sport to rev'lling winds ;
While Sadness sighing sits upon her gates,
Steals 'mid her streets to hear the biting lash,
Veils in our homes the smiles of innocence
That sparkled there to make the fireside heav'n ;
And all Rome's mightiness by heroes nursed,
That panted once to pass this meagre earth,
And strike the stars, down 'neath the heels of Goths
Who gaze around like children on a toy,
Amazed to know from whence their fortune sprang.
And yet Afranius sleeps, and yet Rome sleeps !
Awake ! arouse, and swear with me—revenge !
          [*Exit.*

AFRANIUS.

Stung with the daughter's scorn and father's wrong,
He hurls me forward to assuage his hate.
To slay the Goth at Zala points the sword—
Maybe with her own blood will stain this hand.
Vengeance from Heaven should come and not from
  me.
But must the Goth lash Romans bound with chains ?
Celestial Pow'rs, dispel this madd'ning doubt !

Scene II.—*A retired place in a garden.*

ZALA.

HOW thick the air!

SIBYL.

To me this hour seems bright
And pure as heav'n.   See how the lingering sun,
With orb enlarged, hangs on the horizon's verge,
Fringing with golden hues those western clouds
While all the sky with crimson blushes round !
Oh ! oft on such an eve my fancy spies
The gods with glancing wings and radiant hair
Gliding along those beams of slanted light
From heav'n to earth, and back from earth to
    heav'n.

ZALA.

Sibyl, to me this world is voiceless now ;
My sorrow veils its beauty o'er with gloom.
Believest thou dreams ?

SIBYL.

When Somnus, the dull god,
Shuts in the eye, he wings the soul, whose glance,
With Heav'n's own help, looks through the future's
    mists.

ZALA.

But late, when darkness lay upon the world,
And curtain'd round my couch, while all was still

Save that low sound, like ocean's roar in shells,
Night murmurs in the ear, I wildly dream'd
That I was walking on a toppling cliff
Around whose base of rocks dash'd foam-white
    waves,
When suddenly, seized with a mad desire,
I threw me headlong from the hideous height,
And fell as drops an autumn-shooting star,
Gasping in agony infinite for breath;
Out from their sockets stood mine eyes with pain;
My blood was forced up to my bursting skin,
Until at last I struck the thund'ring surge,
And waked up in the ocean's dark abyss.

         SIBYL.

That wedlock means, unless, defied the Fates,
My charms shall bring thee from engulphing ills.

         ZALA.

Thy secret arts are mysteries to me;
No balm to cure my heart save him I love.

     Enter AFRANIUS.

And here he is, with hope for my despair.
Afranius, save me from rough Jovian's arms!
The King would force me wed him most I hate.
We'll fly to some lone isle where Winter lives,
And tempests dash wild oceans on the rocks;
Our love will tame the storm, and shine our sun,

And garland winter with the bloom of spring;
The vine shall hang her clusters round the spot,
And with the dewy sparkle of the morn
Our songs shall hail the blush upon the hills;
And we will soothe day's monarch to the sea
When twilight brightens with the star of eve.

AFRANIUS.

Thy words cut through my heart—but Heav'n
knows how!

ZALA.

Dost pause! On a mere slave have I exhaled
The virgin fragrance of a loving soul?
Did I mistake a coward for a man,
And deck the fawning wretch with passion's hues?
Dost spurn me off, the daughter of thy king,
To wed a beast whose look and touch I loathe?

AFRANIUS.

Oh! save mine honour, all I have is thine.
'Tis Rome that calls me thus to crush my heart:
Nay! turn each pulsing throb to agony,
And after death pierce with eternal pain.

ZALA.

O man, thy love how prudent and how poor!
I conquer fear for thee; mock death and fate.
A woman's love knows nothing but itself,
And him who has evoked its awful power;
It leaps the bars of wealth, the grades of rank

And thrones of kings; and seas could swim of fire
To clasp its own, and wing eternity.
And nought kills woman's love save woman's pride,
Whose quick o'ermast'ring nature quenches love
As darkness hides the universal day.

AFRANIUS.

Hear me, Zala! hear, I beg thee, hear!

ZALA.

Not words but deeds I want. A *man* would bear
Me on his lion breast along a brink
Of fire where demons yell'd in flames. Farewell!

AFRANIUS.

Oh, Zala, stay! Could I tell all, thyself
Would laud the deed. 'Tis honour spurs me on.

ZALA.

Honour! prate that to fools! a bubble blown
From air that dances in the sun to cheat
Its dupes, whose touch turns back to emptiness.
[*Exit.*

AFRANIUS.

Oh! to be blamed by her who has my heart,
And call'd a coward-slave! 'tis infamy!
This is the piercing pang of misplaced love!
A Roman and a Christian wed a Goth!
Too long this love distill'd ambrosial sweets,
And flush'd my life with dreams, until I've been
As one 'mid ev'ning's music-murm'ring gales

That steal in dalliance where soft summers fringe
A sky-reflecting lake set bright with stars.
Spirit, that fills with flame the patriot's veins,
That drew great Cincinnatus from his plough,
And struck the dagger to Virginia's heart,
Then breathed o'er Livy's page immortal fire,
Come from the past, and help my nerveless arm
Till shines our Rome eternal sun of earth!

ACT III.

Scene I.—*A retired street in Rome.*

VARRO.

Y Lucius, hail! how wrinkled grows thy
brow!
Sad thou as if this world were dead, and thou
Didst stay behind its ashes to inurn.

LUCIUS.

Rome is the world—and is she not a corpse,
Graveless, and foul, fed on by beasts, while ghosts
Shriek round on winds?

ANTONIUS.

And whose but ours the blame
If Jove, with storms, has roll'd mid roaring flames

His chariot from her high-domed Capitol?
He on Olympus sits to mock her sons,
Who, pigmies, strut along her marbled halls
T' amuse the laughing majesty of Heav'n.

VARRO.

Be ours the blame that tears extinguish hope;
Once shone our Rome the jewel of the world,
And kings did beg to be her citizens.

ANTONIUS.

Then we were *men*, and fought till empires ranged
Beneath our sway, and Rome sat on the world,
Proud as her banner'd bird, who from his crag
Looks to the sun, the king of earth and sea.
Oh, now our glory dimm'd and gone our power!
No more the Briton from his ocean-isle,
Chain'd to a swarthy Moor, or Scythian chief,
Follows the victor's car of glittering gold,
Piled with the treasures of a plunder'd world,
And roll'd in triumph to the Capitol;
Instead, Romans in bonds, and lash'd to toil
Where once their fathers with exulting shouts
Bursting from windows, walls, and joyous roofs,
Have rock'd these pillar'd temples to their domes,
And shook th' eternal arches of the heavens.

VARRO.

And would Antonius aid to right our wrongs?

ANTONIUS.
More willing I than serves the hand the head.
LUCIUS.
Thanks to the gods! thy father's fire in thee!
Titanius, with swift words unfold our plans.
TITANIUS.
Yes! we whose fathers sway'd the power of Rome,
Her senates graced, and thunder'd on her fields,
Have sworn to drive these wolves back to their wilds.
ANTONIUS.
Hear I aright? deceives my heart mine ear?
Resolve will burst our chains! 'tis not in words
But wills that Freedom lives! The soul that dares
The tyrant's power, o'erturns the tyrant's throne.
O Rome, in this one oath I hail thee free!
TITANIUS.
Julius, we mock, and yet 'twas he moved first;
The drops from his poor ear have fired our plans;
By him impell'd, we swore to kill each Goth
We meet that day whose feast tells Rome her chains.
Afranius shrank—him Julius yet must swear.
VARRO.
He'll give his hand to break the bonds of Rome:
The breeze that steals on murmuring wing
To kiss the flower, turn'd storm, will shake the world.

TITANIUS.

As coming hither muffled in my cloak,
Old Sibyl placed this parchment in my hand.
                              [*Reads.*

The Fates have sent the earthquake's shock
To heave the hill and rend the rock.
I hear their thunders loud and high!
I see their lightnings o'er the sky!
Red comets blaze, and on the West
Ride warrior-forms for battle dress'd;
With flags of blood they rush, they fight
Till swallow'd up by closing night.
There on the lonely mountain-side
Where Satyrs dance, and demons ride,
The sister Fates amid the gloom
Shriek to the winds Rome's coming doom;
They tell who will the tyrant slay
And live thereafter but a day,
That hero brings to Rome her state
When Glory smiled to make her great.
But if a moment he expires
Before that day has quench'd its fires
Then Rome no more shall gain her might
Until Italia's sons unite
A scarlet Priest to hurl from an imperial height.

ANTONIUS.

Be mine the hour! be mine the envied stroke!

A tyrant there in kingly mantle sits;
There strikes a dagger in a phantom-hand!
Bright visions glorious with immortal shapes
Are smiling round and voices "onward" cry.
Fortune, nor death, nor all an empire's might
Can shake the soul that loves Italia's right;
Be gash'd my body till it bleed and die!
The patriot lives immortal in the sky.

Scene II.—*A private room in Rome.*

AFRANIUS.

HOW sad this hour! Hast ever lost a friend?

JULIUS.

I had no friend save her who gave me life:
Her death made heav'n all cloud, and earth a grave.

AFRANIUS.

Soft as the tear it wakes, the name of friend!
Eve's whispers not so sweet—hence death more drear.
The fate of my Antonius hast thou heard?

JULIUS.

He fail'd, I know, to stab the king, and dies.

AFRANIUS.

He's gone—lone-wandering now amid the shades;
And yet he follows me, stain'd o'er with blood.

JULIUS.

With ghastly look he comes to cry—revenge!
But tell me how he breathed away his ghost.

AFRANIUS.

To deepen the humility of Rome
The tyrant made a gladiatorial show;
And there high-ranged along the circling seats,
Piled, tier o'er tier, the Coliseum round,
These wild Goths saw with Romans Romans fight,
Where once our Pompeys and our Cæsars sat
To see their fathers clubb'd, and torn like beasts;
Barbarians yell while Romans fall to die.

JULIUS.

Each drop of Roman blood for vengeance pleads.

AFRANIUS.

The worst remains; my eye grows dim with tears,
My brain reels round as when a whirlpool boils
While the black horror through my mem'ry swims;
Antonius, hurling defiance at the crowd,
And breathing fiery flashes from his face,
Was dragg'd to view. A Roman stood his foe:
" Perish the hand," he cried, " that here would
    strike!"

JULIUS.

How like Antonius that! What nobleness!

AFRANIUS.

His foe a craven proved: unsheathed his sword,

And flesh'd a biting wound.   In scorn our friend
The wretch disarm'd, and threw him on the sand.
Then shook the Coliseum with the cry
To slip the lion's bars, when, lo ! a beast
With hunger mad and mane erect, rush'd forth,
And stood with glaring eyes, in awful pause,
Till, with a bound, he fasten'd in our friend
Ten horrid claws, and tore him with fierce teeth ;
Blood spouted forth, and he fell on the ground.

JULIUS.

Afranius, kneel, and swear with me revenge !

AFRANIUS.

Vengeance to Heav'n belongs, and not to me.

JULIUS.

Thy colour'd sketches of our ancient Rome,
Thy sickly fancies from thy Christian books,
Thy plunge within the coward-making font,
And thy communings with low vulgar sects
Thy manliness have kill'd.

AFRANIUS.

Thy taunt I bear ;
A world I loathe where only villains win ;
I hate Rome's boasts of blood.   Virtue my aim,
At whose pure shrine bent low the Grecian sage ;
He saw in mists what shines in noon's full sun.
Virtue no more the image of a god
Shaped in cold marble by immortal art,

AFRANIUS.

But our Creator breathing in our flesh;
Divinity come down to talk with men,
To drop a tear for them, and for them die,
Then rise to heav'n a universe to sway.

JULIUS.

Stop thou this stuff, and take the oath from me!

AFRANIUS.

Thou wouldst kill all—wouldst strew our bloody
    streets
With gasping infancy and dying age;
Heav'n can never smile on such dire cruelty.

JULIUS.

Let Heav'n then frown, and Hell cry, death for *all!*
When spared the Goth since yell'd he through our
    gates?
Our city's marr'd by flames; our Romans writhe
Beneath his lash; our children are his slaves;
Our mothers, wives, and daughters in his arms!
Look here, and see mine own deformity!
Each drop from this clipp'd ear says—*all* shall
    die.

AFRANIUS.

Unstain'd by gore shall Rome to glory rise!
No spot on that new crown around her brow
When gleams a cross above her Capitol!

JULIUS.

A sick girl's dream! 'tis blood is freedom's price.

AFRANIUS.
Who seeks the right stands like a radiant god
Whom Heav'n's own hand has arm'd for victory.
I will not swear to slay the innocent!

JULIUS.
Thou shalt!

AFRANIUS.
Shalt?

JULIUS.
Aye, shalt!

AFRANIUS.
Shalt! do thou beware!

JULIUS.
Do thou, not I, beware! I would not rouse
The lion from his lair to feel his fang;
A brawl between us is the death of Rome.
Let me proclaim that Zala has thine heart,
And on my witness place your whisper'd vows,
Thee Goths would kill, and madden'd Romans curse;
Two walls of circling flames close o'er thy head.

AFRANIUS.
Oh, shall this scheming over-master me!
Ye lofty notions of immortal truth
By Heav'n inspired, must ye bend now to craft?
Must virtue wither in a villain's breath?
My Zala or my Rome through me must die.

JULIUS.

Tell me if thou wilt swear to kill the Goth!

AFRANIUS.

I swear.

JULIUS.

All?

AFRANIUS.

All!

JULIUS.

All on the feast-day met?

AFRANIUS.

I swear.

JULIUS.

One spared, or old or young, is death.
Hence mercy bid farewell, and steel thine heart!
[*Exit.*

AFRANIUS.

Alone in night, no guiding hand to clasp!
Love draws me here, and there my country calls;
The shadow of a doubt on all my life!
One bold bad man will gain his evil end
Before the good, perplex'd, can leave his knees.
Oh, Heaven, look down, and smile upon my deed;
But led by Thee I'll go through this thick night;
Beyond smiles Truth in her eternal light.

ACT IV.

Scene I.—*A banqueting hall in a Palace. The
King at the head of the table; Gothic courtiers
around.*

KING.

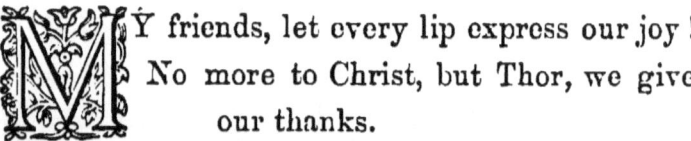Y friends, let every lip express our joy!
No more to Christ, but Thor, we give
our thanks.
This feast recalls the hour when our brave Goths
Seized Rome's proud eagle which had awed a world,
And clipp'd his plumes with their victorious
swords.

FIRST GOTH.

First to our gods we brimming goblets fill!

[*All drink.*

SECOND GOTH.

Next, to our warrior-shades we quaff our wine!
Our fathers fed with blood the eye of Rome;
Their sons have seen her lords with wild beasts
fight.

[*All drink.*

KING.

Blind Fate rules Thor himself, and sinks in dust,

Or lifts amid the clouds—to Fate we drink.
　　　　　　　　　　　　　[*All drink.*
Let song now fling all shadows from the soul!
　　　　　ALL SING.
　　To Thor, to Thor, to Thor
　　Send up the shout of war!
　　To Thor, to Thor our cry
　　When battle fires the sky!
　　To Thor the war-spoils bring,
　　And round red altars sing!
　　　　　THIRD GOTH.
But why, O King, this paleness on thy cheek?
What airy shape doth fix thy straining eye?
　　　　　KING.
A shadow, but a shadow—there, 'tis pass'd!
Let music drive its darkness from my brain!
　　　　　ALL SING.
As the wine of the feast gives its strength to the eye,
As our battle-swords flash their red light o'er the
　　sky,
'Tis the victor of Jove, our own Thor we behold,
Him who tore from the Cæsar his purple and gold.
　　　　　KING.
Thor conquer'd Christ and Jove, and hence my god.
His thunders loud! the air is quivering flame!
Hell seems with Heaven to fight and get my soul;
The peal, the flash to me are ominous.

FOURTH GOTH.

Nay! Heav'n is telling that its clouds drop rain
To make the golden crops and mellow fruits,
And give its joyous sparkle to the wine.

KING.

The pang is gone—drain now the brimming cups
To drown these cares that grin about our throne,
And pierce like thorns the head that wears a crown.

FIRST GOTH.

To Alaric, who first our banner waved
Above the Capitol, and sleeps now safe
In coffin'd gold beneath Busentinus!

                                                 [*All drink.*

KING.

I will the casement seek, and court the winds
Of Heaven to play on my quick-throbbing brow.

                                 [*Aside at the window.*

Some spirit spreads black wings upon the night,
And breathes a subtle poison through the air.
Away these images from memory!
My soul is like yon cloud that hangs o'er Rome
To hide the stars, while torches flash below,
And fill the spectral sky with lurid glare.

SECOND GOTH.

To peerless Zala, royal rose of Rome!
May north and south alike love her sweet bloom!

                                                 [*All drink.*

KING.

Zala, ye said! that word brings back my dreams!
The red moon rides amid the flying clouds,
While fountains spout beneath in streams of blood,
Leaping through air in demon mockery!
A shrouded matron from an altar tears
A queenly bride whose voice shrieks out our
    fall!
Tempestuous shouts now pierce my aching ear
Like screams of drowning men out on the sea,
Above the storm and thunder of the wave!
Away these shows of joy! this emptiness!
Why deck my death-bed with the flowers of
    spring?
Why spread a feast beside my yawning grave?
Heaven speaks in fire, and earth casts up her dead!

Enter Messengers.

FIRST MESSENGER.

Excuse my homage, King, and hear my words!
Our Roman slaves on by Afranius led—
    KING (*striking him to the floor*).
Ill-omen'd owl, I'll stop thy boding voice!
Ye gods, how writhes the knave like some trod
    worm!

SECOND MESSENGER.

I fear, O king, my news will cost my life!

KING.

Speak out! the storm has pass'd, and now my veins
Beat like an infant's pulse.

SECOND MESSENGER.

By Julius stirr'd,
And by Afranius led, and bound by oaths
To kill each Goth they meet, the Roman slaves
Have arm'd, and shed our blood, and fire our homes.

KING.

Quick, fly, my friends, while I defend my throne!
[*Exeunt all but* KING.
Julius, thy mother's blood spots o'er this hand,
And thou, unconscious, dost avenge the stain.
The eye of Heav'n is on the murd'rer's track;
Not for a guilty king his throne a shield!
Omnipotence would drag me up from hell,
Or pluck me from the stars to meet my fate!
Rage on, ye storms! ye thunders, peal my doom!
I feel beneath my feet a tott'ring throne!

Enter AFRANIUS.

Ha! serpent, is it thou? I thought not this!
My love to thee requited with thy sword!

AFRANIUS.

Thou art the foe of Rome, and hence must die.

KING.

I strike thee, slave!

[*The* KING *rushes at* AFRANIUS, *but after a struggle is killed.*

AFRANIUS (*over the body*).

My hate gash'd not that flesh
On which these tears drop down in agony;
'Twas love for thee, Itália, pierced this king;
Else murder's stain would be eternal here.
Rebellion, oh, most terrible thy front,
Though shaped by Heav'n's own hand, and from
    the sleep
Of calm endurance by an angel waked
To put the mantle of thy terrors on,
And ride the whirlwind; for thy path is blood,
Groans are thy music, and thy breath is flame:
Thou dost to death-pangs turn the infant's smile,
While o'er her cold dead babe the mother weeps.
Nay, at thy feet I see my Zala lie,
Pale on her face the light of woman's love.
O Liberty, thy price such blood, and yet
Humanity must burst each tyrant's chain!

Enter ZALA (*pursued by* JULIUS *with a drawn dagger*).

ZALA.

Save me, my love! Save, oh, save me!

AFRANIUS.

Back, slave,

On thy life! back, or thou shalt die!
JULIUS.

Ha! caught,
Afranius, caught! Fate is too strong for faith!
There cries to thee thy love, and here thy oath!
Thy heart and honour have now join'd in war;
Kill thou this girl, or perjure thine own soul!
AFRANIUS.
Incarnate Mercy could not cleanse the spot!
ZALA.
I bare my breast to thee! drain out each drop,
And with my blood pay down thine honour's price!
AFRANIUS.
I will obey my heart, and not my head,
And trust that Heav'n will smile away my sin.
JULIUS.
Then mine the blow—my hand pays off the score:
Now with her life I will avenge mine ear!

[JULIUS *attempts to stab* ZALA. AFRANIUS, *seizing him, throws him violently down.*

AFRANIUS (*stooping to examine the body*).
The villain's pulse is still! Zala, we fly.

ZALA (*pointing to the* KING).
Behold these eyes that stare into thy face,
These lips compress'd in their last agony,
This drooping head, these cold and nerveless limbs,

These wounds which murder shriek ! thy friend's,
    thy king's !
A father's corpse lies there between our hearts.

AFRANIUS.

Forgive the blow ! 'twas Heav'n's high will, not
    mine;
A month will find my power firm in our Rome,
And then I will proclaim thee as my wife.

ZALA.

That blood has left a spot no rite can purge.

AFRANIUS.

If Heav'n blots out my sin, why wilt not thou ?
In some old temple I can hide thee safe
Until this tempest passes from our path.

ZALA.

Ne'er can Hope bind her halo round our lives;
The past may fringe my sorrows with its light,
But not its golden ray can chase my gloom ;
A crimson sea divides love cannot cross ;
My life a stain on thine—each heart-throb here
Within this breast proclaims thy broken vow.
This glittering dagger, snatch'd when Havoc's
    cry
Wild-hurtling through the air our palace reach'd,
Will be my passport to elysian fields
Where I to thee will glide made pure by death,
And spend eternal ages in thy love.

AFRANIUS.
This is no time for words, I bear thee off.
                  [*Exit with* ZALA *in his arms.*
         JULIUS (*slowly rising*).
Kill'd, not yet! no thanks to thee, Afranius!
But, dead, my soul would wander bodiless
To mar thy bliss. Thy fireside should grow dark,
When jealousy's sharp thorn in thee I'd plant,
And breathe suspicion on the treach'rous air,
Till Zala's beauty seem'd deformity;
Her breast of love cold as the mountain's crown;
Loathsome her touch; a harlot's trick her kiss.
Spurning this king, her blood and thine I'll have;
Remorseless Fate draws round her tight'ning folds!
Bright as the morning now may smile your skies,
Yet from this broken oath a storm shall grow
Blacker than night, and charged for both with
    death.

SCENE II.—*Temple of Apollo in Rome.* SIBYL *engaged in her incantations.*

YE gods who from the azure hills look down
   To trace the thoughts that weave our
      destiny,
Watching each charm as girlish beauty bursts
To womanhood, and ye who manhood guard,

Leading its eagle-wing up to the sun
That it may soar where coward-natures sink,
Alas, grim darkness o'er your children scowls,
And Julius vengeful stalks amid the gloom.
Encircled in this scroll, their mystic fate,
While yet my oath forbids to break the seal!
I'll stand upon the temple's eastern porch,
And Phœbus as he lifts his face of fire
Above the hills may show the token wish'd. [*Exit.*

Enter AFRANIUS *and* ZALA *from opposite parts.*

AFRANIUS.

Come to my arms! the vail lifts from our lives!
The drop baptismal glitt'ring on thy brow
Stood sparkling there a prophet of new joy.

ZALA.

When I before the Cross renounced our gods
The wall between our hearts itself fell down;
Our mingled lives shall flow from earth to heav'n.

AFRANIUS.

Where once night-brooding doubt sat on my life
And turn'd stern action to abortive thought,
Faith like an angel smiles and bids me on.
To do, or bear, or die, alike to us,
Since Heav'n, we know, unwinds our destiny.

ZALA.

Like some full cup whose sparkling drops brim
  o'er,

My heart o'erflows with joy—but thou must fly.
See, Julius peers around that column's base!

JULIUS (*appearing*).

Afranius, duped again; I'm not yet dead,
But live to blast thy love, thy name, thy life.

AFRANIUS.

Hell is unlock'd to belch thee from its flames.

ZALA.

Ye pillars of yon dome, oh, crush the wretch!
What is thine errand here?

JULIUS.

                Canst thou not tell?
Thy father maim'd me thus and died; by whom?
The hand of him, my tool, whom most I loathe.

ZALA.

This not enough?

JULIUS.

        'Tis much, not all I ask.
Crush'd by contempt, love turns to brooding hate,
Waking the keenest of all mortal pangs
That gnaw till death will keep from rival arms.

AFRANIUS.

Man yet in form, a demon hast thou turn'd!

JULIUS.

Afranius, thou hast won the heart I loved;
Need I tell thee how for this I hate thee?

A blow from thy clench'd fist fell on me here;
Each hour it burns, and tingles in my nerves,
And boils along the channels of my blood,
And, mounting to my brain, it crazes me.
                              [*Shouting heard.*
Ha! ye are mine! Our Romans fill the place,
And cry out for his blood who broke his oath.

Enter Soldiers.

Drag this weak traitor to a felon's death!

AFRANIUS.

Nay! ye minions, back! I am Afranius!
This voice rang out amid the clash of arms;
This hand flung first your banner to the winds,
And slew the tyrant in his palace-hall.
Him will ye kill who struck your fetters off,
And pay back with his blood the debt ye owe?
Stand! I say, stand, and hold my person sacred!
I'll come before your judges in an hour,
And answer then the charges ye may urge;
But not with pinion'd hands and head droop'd down
While the vile rabble hoots behind my back.
Nay! I will walk as now, towering and firm,
With the bold tread of manly innocence
And conscious service render'd to the state,
And prove upon my side humanity.
Ye Romans are! respect me, too, a Roman!

ACT V.

Scene I.—*A temple of Jupiter.*

SIBYL.

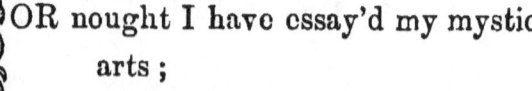OR nought I have essay'd my mystic
    arts;
My prayers are useless, and my spells
    are vain;
Or anger'd are the gods, or has old age
My powers benumb'd, and dimm'd my baffled eyes?
On every side teem signs I may not read;
The arrowy swallows from their chimney-tops,
Majestic swans that o'er their shadows swim,
With vultures circling up till specks they seem
Across the white of clouds; and wars on earth,
And blazing battles o'er the fiery sky,
I scan in vain, nor make the future out.
Yet Hope will see these pillars rise around,
Yon dome arch'd o'er, while breathing marbles line
With forms of life again these lonely aisles,
And once more *Romans* on these pavements kneel.
Immortal Jove, come here from yonder cloud!
Ah! sailing o'er its fringe of silver'd light,
Then lost to view, thine eagle's form I see;
Gleaming in lightning-fires he sweeping comes

And cleaves with his broad breast the stormy air!
Flashes thy thundering bolt to strike thy bird!
He shrieking falls and with him falls our Rome!
Broad opens now the future to my sight
Where Havoc blasts, and Rome sinks down in
    night!

Scene II.—*The Roman* Forum. Varro, Lucius, *and* Titanius *robed as Judges;* Afranius *and* Zala *standing as accused;* Julius *as Prosecutor.*

                  VARRO.

PRIS'NERS! are ye prepared?
                  AFRANIUS.
              We are, my Lords!
                  VARRO.

Then let these shouts be hush'd, nor Justice lift
Her beam where storms thus roar. The charge
    ye know!
                  AFRANIUS.

And stand to meet!
                  VARRO.
            A Roman shall have right.
                  AFRANIUS.

Our sole defence is in the very deed.

VARRO.

Julius, stand forth, and state what thou wilt urge.

JULIUS.

I charge he broke his oath which bound to kill
Each Goth he met on the high festal day.

VARRO.

The proofs produce! nay, the most certain proofs.
Without sure proofs, through us, no Roman dies.

JULIUS.

Ye judges, hear! I'll give what ye demand.
That night of massacre I sought this girl,
Who saw me, and wild-shrieking ran away.
Enraged, with dagger drawn, I follow'd her;
She flew along the hall, and like a fawn
Sped on from room to room, till, urged by fate,
She saw Afranius o'er her father's corpse,
And scream'd for help. I shouted out, "Thy
    oath!"
He hurl'd me down and bore the girl away,
A refuge making near Apollo's shrine,
As all these Romans know, who seized them there.
Now I or he, I claim, must kill this girl,
And, if his hand refuse, he too must die.

VARRO.

Not hate, but justice, should thy words inspire.

JULIUS.

I am not here for right, but for revenge!

This blazes through my veins, and burns my brain—
Stung by his blow, disfigured by her sire,
I only live to quench my hate in blood.
VARRO.
Afranius, speak in answer to this charge.
AFRANIUS.
My lords, he owns that malice brought him here,
Nor hides his hate beneath the forms of law,
But flaunts it hideous to the day's broad glare.
I broke my oath, and glory in the deed,
Since, gain'd its end, its binding force was gone,
And then to kill had mark'd with murder's stain.
VARRO.
Admit not aught to prejudice your cause.
AFRANIUS.
I ask not my own life! nay, ask to die!
But why condemn this girl, whose blood would be
A stain eternal on the name of Rome?
She cries through me to save from yon crazed
    wretch
Whose nostril now dilates with smell of blood.
There is a golden line by Heav'n inscribed
To stay the law's rash steps—'tis Charity.
Nor is our state yet firm; the northman's fires
Will blaze along these hills that stand round Rome;
His trumpets peal, his armies seek revenge.
With useless murder then incense him not.

Your judgment we await!

VARRO (*after consultation by the Judges*).

Our duty plain!
Afranius has confessed his oath he broke,
And hence compels us to pronounce his death—
Unless he kill the girl.

AFRANIUS.

My Lords, ye mock.
On life's verge poised, will ye insult me there?
Am I a thief round whom the rabble yell—
A wretch whose honour as his robe sits loose,
And who would sell his manhood for his breath,
Piercing the heart he loved to save his life?
If this ye think of me, I beg to die!

VARRO.

To save thy life, we strain'd for thee the law;
Mercy refused, thy death is thine own deed.

AFRANIUS.

My lords, I know I've dream'd—dream'd of a time
When Rome should win a brighter glory back
Than flash'd from vict'ry 'neath her eagle's eye
To shape her marbles, and inspire her song;
When breathed her orators heroic fire,
And swarm'd her streets till beat here earth's
great heart.
I when a boy have climb'd yon Capitol
To read in stony lips and eyes her wrongs,

While waving in the moon the ivy sigh'd,
And spirits groan'd to stars their grief that Rome
Should feel despair eternal at her heart.
Like some spired city o'er a dusky plain,
Oft through the future's darkness rose to view
Resplendent visions of her olden fame.
Death paints another scene before my sight.
Crown'd on these hills, with crook shall rule a
    Priest
In scarlet robed, and claiming to be God;
Where thund'ring legions bore our eagles on
He shall with monks a second empire build,
Whose spoil is souls, whose traffic Mercy's blood,
Whose power, not swords, but Heav'n's own
    barter'd keys.
Beyond his reign, prophetic years will come
To shed upon the earth millennial bloom;
And yet, beyond, a city bursts to view
Whose streets are gold, whose walls far-flashing
    gems;
Its sun His Face divine who died for man,
And rules Creation as Eternal king.
    ZALA *(tearing away her veil)*.
Afranius, thou must live!
    AFRANIUS.
        On yonder cloud
An angel smiles, and calls us to the skies.

ZALA (*rushing and kneeling before the Judges*).
Hear me, ye judges, and ye men of Rome!
Me make the victim which your laws demand!
Mar not his form, nor let your axe distain
That brow which Fame and Freedom both entwine!

VARRO.

Lictors, proceed, and lead them to the block!

ZALA (*kneeling before* AFRANIUS).

'Tis I have call'd this stroke down on thine head!
Let, then, on me the blow of Justice fall!
The state ordains, and hence 'tis law, not crime.
Oh, cut earth's ties! I'll gain celestial wings,
And soon our souls will meet, and we in light
Will trace the windings of Life's groves and
    streams,
And thrill with love eternal to our King!

Enter SIBYL.

SIBYL.

Make room! make room! and hear the gracious
    gods!

VARRO.

Sibyl, thy looks some message tell from Heav'n!

SIBYL.

My age and name are proofs of what I say.
Julius, thy mother on the couch of death
This parchment gave, and till the gods should speak

AFRANIUS.   57

She made me swear to never break the seal.
Just now within the temple of great Jove
I heard a voice in awful thunders say—
" Fly, to the judges fly, and give the scroll!"
Then silence settled in the solemn place.
   [VARRO *taking the scroll, the Judges read*
     it and consult.

VARRO.

This is an interference from the gods,
As, Romans, all your judges do affirm.

CITIZENS.

The scroll! the scroll! tell us what says the
 scroll!

VARRO.

An infant of the king, a girl, expired,
And from the breast of her who Julius bore
The former Queen took Zala as her child.
A Roman thus, and not within the oath,
Your judges do pronounce th' accused are free.

JULIUS.

A shallow lie to rob me of revenge!
   [AFRANIUS *and* ZALA *embrace amid the*
    shouts of the people.
Oh! hated sight more sharp than pangs of hell!
Worse than the tooth of Cerberus that kiss!
That bliss I'll blast, and take eternal fire.
   [JULIUS, *rushing, stabs* AFRANIUS.

AFRANIUS.

Oh! fatal stab that robs of Love and Rome!
Death darkens o'er mine eyes and earth swims
    round!
Zala, thy face shines like the star of eve,
And Life immortal bursts on all my gloom!
    [AFRANIUS *dies, and* ZALA, *falling, expires on*
    his body.

SIBYL.

Ye gods, had he but breathed till set yon sun,
In him had lived for us Eternal Rome!
Hope made me blind! Jove's bolt was prophecy!

VARRO.

Lictors, the murd'rer seize, and hold him fast!

JULIUS.

Hands off, ye men of Rome! I'll cheat you all,
And spoil your vengeance with this dagger's point!
    [JULIUS *stabs himself and dies.*

SIBYL.

Where I divined new glory for our Rome,
The voice was heard through Jove's majestic
    aisles
That I might snatch these from a felon's death,
And give their names immortal to the stars.
Oh, long 'mid gloom shall Rome in scarlet sit,
The nations ruling with a priestly hand,
And empires luring on the path of death

By the false glitter on her ghostly brow!
But now on these old eyes new brightness streams,
Nor kings nor pontiffs shine beneath its beams;
Italia! when thy capital is Rome,
Eternal glory then shall burst o'er Freedom's home!

ARISTON.

ARISTON.

ACT I.

SCENE I.—*A room in Athens in which a symposium has just been finished.*

ARISTIPPUS.

IOLO, hold him—hold him lest he fall!
Our common manhood sinks in him
to earth.

PHILIPPON.

Jove, how the fellow reels, yet heavy seems,
And helpless as the dead!

ARISTIPPUS.

Ariston, stand!
Stand like a man and be once more thyself!
No overloaded ship out on the sea,
When struck by storms and waves, would stagger
so.

IOLO.

How beautiful for Greece the bound where wine
Will sparkles give to wit, not madd'ning flames!

PHILIPPON.

Our gods implore to never crown our feasts,
Since, if none touch, none thus can turn to beasts.

ARISTIPPUS.

Cease thy philosophy, and lend thine hand!
Our strength is vain.   [ARISTON *falls*.
            Our friend is down once more—
Down like a Satyr, snoring off his cups.

IOLO.

Athens ne'er show'd a form or soul so fine—
Yet her Hyperion dribbles on the floor
—The lustre gone from two half-open'd eyes,
Vacant and red—a face that look'd a god's
Most pitifully blank—a head and limbs
Whence Phidias took the majesty of Jove,
Immortal making his Olympian king,
Lie low together in that heap of flesh
—A slave to wine the soul that might read
            stars,
Rule over men, and strike from states their bonds!

Enter CALOPHOS.

CALOPHOS.

Oh! worse than death this sight—a corpse less sad

Whose worms proclaim our doom, than mind
  debased!
IOLO.
Behold thy work—the end of thy wise ways—
The pride of thy free school down there a slave!
CALOPHOS.
I ask why men earth's bounty thus will curse?
The cause of drunkenness, I say, is one.
ARISTIPPUS.
Nay! this man loves his wine to wing his wit:
And that to warm his blood, or gild his gloom.
IOLO.
This friend, rotund, imbibes, as sponges, dews;
That, lean, like some old pipe when summer suns
Have touch'd earth's gracious springs, and made
  them low.
PHILIPPON.
Ariston is the type and sum of all.
Immortal Bacchus 'tis makes mortals reel;
Olympus drunk, the earth will stagger more.
CALOPHOS.
Youth is the steed that whirls the car to wreck
Where age will drive as silent as its rein.
What earth of good could give, Ariston had
The spark of genius flash'd out from his eyes,
And Athens half adored her godlike son;
Yet in his soul the void that cries for wine,

And in man's shame shows kinship to the gods.
   [*While* CALOPHOS *is speaking,* ARISTON, *arising,*
     seizes an immense flagon and drops into it
     a maddening drug.

IOLO.

If thou be right, yon flagon makes him Jove!

CALOPHOS.

Be quick! and hold his hand!

PHILIPPON.

                    Wine proves us gods!
Then let him drink, and plume immortal wings!

CALOPHOS.

Ariston, stop! 'tis fire for thee and death!
That drug burns to his blood, and makes him
   mad!
Wrench quick the flagon from his clutch and lip!
      [*They rush at* ARISTON, *who resists, and*
         drives them off.

ARISTON.

Master, I heard thy words. Hail, sparkling cup!
Bright proof that we immortals yet shall be,
'Tis heav'n itself that flashes in thy gleam!
Wise Calophos, thy thoughts have sober'd me;
Thou magic wine, gay daughter of the sun,
Whose own paternal rays thy virtues dart,
That man may share the nectar of the gods,
Who says a serpent coils round in thy cup,

To sting my sense, and reason blast, and joy?
Nay! 'tis Olympus bubbles on thy brim.
Calophos, I drink to thy philosophy!
> [*They again seek to prevent* ARISTON, *who succeeds in draining the flagon, and is excited after the struggle into frenzy.*

ARISTON.

Immortal gods! my head whirls round in fire!
Put out these flames that blaze around my flesh,
Crawl o'er my hair, and twist and hiss like snakes
Oh, help ye! water! help, and quench this fire!

> [HELIA, *the mother of* ARISTON, *enters, silently takes his hand, and subdues him at once.*

ARISTON.

Mother, I own thy spell! Thy look of love
Goes to my heart and cools my burning brain!
Lead where thou wilt, and I will follow thee!
No words! no words! Thy silence rules my soul,
And speech but maddens me!

> [*Exit* HELIA *leading her son by the hand.*

CALOPHOS.

                          Maternal Love!
More is thy magic than philosophy!
Where reason fails, thy touch the tiger tames.
Love, thou art stronger than immortal truth,
And, when states built by force lie ghastly wrecks
Thou wilt in hearts earth's final empire throne!

SCENE II.—*A room in* ALCANDER'S *house at Athens.*
ALCANDER.

 BROTHER, Athens cannot be so base;
Her honours on my brow for twice ten
years
Are proofs she knows how much she owes my love.

HEROCLES.

Thy love of her, Alcander, or thyself?
Hast thou not lived and blossom'd on the state,
And hung thy family tree with flow'rs and fruits?
Democracies are quick to read men through,
And weigh what they deserve of good or ill,
While often envy hurls their idols down.

ALCANDER.

Herocles, thou art bold, I think too bold.
Athens will never dare to frown on me;
If she prove false, I'll pay her back tenfold.

HEROCLES.

Ha! this thy love! The tiger feed, a child
May stroke his skin; keep back his meat, he glares,
And shows his fangs.

ALCANDER.

Such insults I'll not bear;
Nor shall the mob exile me with the shell.

All the best blood of Greece is in our veins,
And from the gods themselves our pedigree.
Thrice round my brow the crown has hung its
    leaves,
While shook the Agora with shouts that moved
Athena throned on her Acropolis.

HEROCLES.

The mountain-tree invites the thunderbolt,
Which blazes harmless o'er the modest vales.
Athens, Alcander,—hast thou not yet learn'd?—
Just where she most exalts she most suspects.
Shrill envy hisses in her wildest praise;
Her hand binds on the crown to tear it off;
Her noblest worth she dooms to banishment
The warmer her embrace the blow more sure.

ALCANDER.

Curse on her mobs! they'll find in me their match.
The snake, untouch'd, will slumber in his coil,
But, struck, darts venom through the quiv'ring
    flesh.

HEROCLES.

Thy threats but prove thy heart to Greece most
    false;
True love to her has not its life in self,
Seeks not its own, o'er pride exalts the State,
And, like a tree whose shatter'd length lies low,
Will from old roots lift high new boughs to heav'n.

ALCANDER.

I've been a fool! duped by the crowd's vile breath.
Fortune across my sky has beam'd so bright
That I will madden in the shades of night.

HEROCLES.

Who mounts on clouds towards the gilding sun
Will see his painted splendors turn to air,
And drop 'mid crowds, who yell to see him fall.

ALCANDER.

Help me, ye gods, and keep me from such wreck!
Yes! all earth's blessings leave behind a gloom,
As sculptured figures crown'd with grace and light
Cast spectral shadows in the brilliant sun.

HEROCLES.

Thou art indeed above a precipice;
Thy birth and dignities will bring the blow.
Thy head made for a king, thy spurning foot
And flashing eye awake the crowd's distrust.
The men thy name who shout thine exile mean,
And thee unmake to show from *them* the power
Which Fame as thine doth trumpet o'er the world.

ALCANDER.

Let Persia, then, fix firm her throne in Greece!
Better one king than a vile tyrant crowd.

HEROCLES.

The people know thy heart inclines thee there,
And thee the shell will drive to live with kings.

ARISTON.   71

Yet those, mere children in the Agora,
Upon the battle-field are matchless men,
Who Attica have wall'd with adamant,
And Asia's banner'd tyrants have defied.,
Our Athens shines the type of that bright day
When they who own the State the State shall sway.

Enter Servants, *bearing* ARISTON *on a litter, stupefied after his debauch, and covered with a robe.*

ALCANDER.

Stop, knaves! what bear ye there?

FIRST SERVANT.

We may not tell.

ALCANDER.

Tell, rascals, tell! at once take off that robe!

SECOND SERVANT.

Oh, master, pause! the sight will stir thy rage!

ALCANDER.

Thou slave, obey!

[*The* Servants *draw aside the robe.*

'Tis that doth pierce my pride.
Our house's blot! Mine image on that wretch!
My pedigree brought down from gods to brutes!
Take, take the breathing infamy away!

Enter HELIA.

HELIA.

My Lord, relent!

ALCANDER.

Helia, behold *thy* son,
His features turn'd to loathsomeness by wine!
From thee, not me, the taint that mars our name.

HELIA.

His only hold on virtue is our love:
But cut that tie, and he will live accursed.

ALCANDER.

Once, ivy-crown'd, before the Parthenon,
Whose pillar'd majesty might awe a beast,
I saw him with his thyrsus chasing boys,
Who mock'd the staggering wretch and me his sire.

HELIA.

All mortals frail should weep when mortals sin;
How, then, should parents bathe with tears a son?

ALCANDER.

His presence in our house will madden me.

HELIA (*kneeling before* ALCANDER).

Let pity move thy breast! Recall thy kiss
First press'd on his sweet lips, the light on thee
From his joy-sparkling eye, the dimpling smile
Which stirr'd thy father's heart, the prattled word
Whose music-thrill awaked new worlds of love;
His childhood's beauty, and his boyhood's morn;
His manhood's glory which Apollo's seem'd,
And moved to say—" There goes the pride of
    Greece!"

Oh, save our son and bind him to thy heart!
Exalting him, Alcander, lift thyself,
And kindle for our house from gloom a light.
Thy life beats in his blood—his soul from thee,
And manly majesty, which mirrors thine;
By thee cast off, he wanders to despair.

ALCANDER.

My heart is touch'd, and yet I fear thy plea;
Expell'd our roof, we purge off his disgrace.

HELIA.

Oh, what can stop a mother's words of love!
I kneel between my son and utter woe,
One hand in his, the other clasping thine,
And am 'twixt him and thee a link of life.
I kiss thy feet, and bathe them with my tears.
Oh, in his haggard face I beauty see
Come back, and hope and love shed o'er their
    light.
He yet shall be the glory of our state,
And where he goes, to live or die, I go:
With kisses on his lips I seal my vow.

HEROCLES.

A mother's cry, Alcander, should be heard;
The gods speak to thee in these touching tears.

ALCANDER.

Once more I yield; but my last weakness this;
His next offence shall drive him from my roof;

We'll leave him till he sleeps away his wine.
[*The* Servants *place the robe over* ARISTON, *who,
when all have left, arises.*

ARISTON.

Her tones of love have brought me to myself.
A tranquil glory lingers round this spot,
Like beams when radiant gods leave earth for heav'n.
A presence here, that bathes me in its light,
My manhood wakes, and gilds my future o'er.
Oh, matchless magic of a mother's love,
Which sees in midnight day, hope in despair,
In death itself the promise of new life,
And him whom Heav'n gives o'er wins back with
    tears.
O man, thy heart how cold, how sharp, how hard!
'Tis ice, 'tis stone, 'tis steel, 'tis adamant,
While woman's love will soften Pluto's realm!

Enter CALOPHOS.

Master, hast thou thine angel ever seen?

CALOPHOS.

'Tis to my soul and not mine eye he speaks.
When I in darkness sink beneath life's load,
A whisper shows my path, a hand clasps mine
To hold me up, and light shines on my steps.

ARISTON.

My guide is flesh'd, is seen, is touch'd, is heard;

A shape which glides in beauty to my side,
To drop a tear, and then like virtue smile.

CALOPHOS.

Is this thy jest?

ARISTON.

Not so, my Calophos;
In thee I own a power that lifts thee up,
And helps thee climb where others blinded crawl—
A Guide invisible who leads thee on.

CALOPHOS.

'Tis true as that there is a voice in winds,
In light a life that folds our world with bloom,
Or that in man which yearns to ever be.

ARISTON.

Dost thou remember, Calophos, the day,
When in the fight, beneath my boyish arm,
Nine soldiers fell, and lay piled round in heaps,
Helm upon helm, and shield on shatter'd shield,
While I stood wounded on the slipp'ry ground,
My corselet cleft, a spear thrust in my breast,
O'er all my armour blood, and reel'd my brain
And steps? Now in mine ear that battle-roar—
Now swift I see thee come, strike right and left,
Then snatch me from my foes, and bear me off,
As Troy's great hero saved his sire from flames.

CALOPHOS.

My back can feel thee now press on it sore!

Jove! how thy dangling legs struck on my heels,
As, breathless, I went stagg'ring 'neath my load!
ARISTON.
Well, Calophos, not in that thick of death,
That clash of meeting swords, that ring of
    shields,
The tramp, the groans, the shouts of battle's hell,
Where ghosts flew shrieking o'er the pain and
    blood,
Was I so weak, so lost, as here and now.
I am a slave—a mean, ignoble slave—
Slave to myself—slave to the foe I hate.
I vow to break my chain, and tighten it;
I curse the cup, and press it to my lips;
I loathe the serpent's cold and snaky coil,
Yet clasp it round my flesh! the fang invite
Whose poison-fire burns in my madden'd brain,
To wake its hissing phantoms twisting round.
But a new strength is in me, Calophos!
Not from thy words, though wise; not from thy
    school,
Whose fame will gild o'er time; not from our
    gods,
Whose revels make Olympus worse than earth.
Spurning the laws of custom and of sex,
My Mother's Love has search'd me in my haunts;
In crowd and street has lifted me from earth,

ARISTON. 77

To thrill me with its touch, its tone, its look,
Till in my flesh its virtue seems infused,
And through my soul a power above mine own
By which I know I yet shall be a man.

Scene III.—*A Banqueting-room in Athens; the guests, garlanded, recline around the table;* Ariston *presiding.*

IOLO.

ARISTON, folly 'tis to make a feast,
And touch no cup,—Athens will laugh at thee.

PHILIPPON.

To Cupid drink, or on thy festal throne
He'll strike thee howling with a thistle-spear;
And bees will leave their bloom to sting thee off.

ARISTIPPUS.

To Bacchus drink, or he'll draw out thy ears;
Old Pan shall stride thy back, and with his hoofs
Punch in thy sides, while Fauns and Dryads pierce
With swords of thorn, and twist thee round with vines.

ARISTON.

Excuse me, friends! I pray this once, excuse!

IOLO.

Ariston, nay! quick! pledge us in a cup!

ARISTON (*pours out some wine and holds it before
a lamp*).
I would not cloud, my friends, our festival,
And yet ye drive me into serious words.
        PHILIPPON.
Ariston, cease, nor cast round us thy gloom!
        ARISTON.
How bright this cup! Behold, its sparkles dance
And flash their joy! Oh, burns my thirsting lip
But for a drop! My soul grows mad to rush
And quench its flames, and lose in wine its woe;
Yet there an adder coils whose sting is death,
And sleeping there may lie eternal pangs.
My friends, one slightest sip would ruin me;
Would set my blood on fire, palsy my will,
And craze my brain, till I a fiend would rave.
I will not touch, but triumph o'er myself,
And feel the manhood of a conquering soul.
Now see before your eyes how hard for slaves
From Pleasure's gilded chains to burst away!

    [*Persons representing the deities of Greece enter.
    JUPITER OLYMPIUS, with his sceptre, takes his
    throne, his eagle at his feet, and at his side
    JUNO, under a rainbow, with her peacock. On
    one side stand BACCHUS, VENUS, and CUPID,
    with PAN, and his Fauns and Satyrs, while no*

the other are APOLLO, DIANA, *and* MARS, *with
the Muses, Nymphs, and Graces.*

JUPITER.

The majesty of heav'n and earth, I come
To hear your songs, and victory award.
I, who Olympus rule and deathless gods,
Grasp here my thunderbolt, while at my feet
Yon kingly bird, whose gaze is o'er the world,
Type of my high and universal sway.
Juno, my queen, sits, glitt'ring round with light,
While that bright thing of eyes, in colours gay,
Stands by her side, and her omniscience shows.
First, Bacchus, thine immortal song we'll hear !

BACCHUS.

When young Spring breathes and curls the vine,
   I watch its root;
   And bud and shoot,
And grape and mantling leaf are mine.
From trunk to twig I make glad juices run,
Till glows the landscape purpling in the sun.

 Now Fauns and Satyrs sing, and bless !
   Pan, tune thy pipe !
   The world is ripe ;
 Those hanging clusters pull and press !
Around the earth let bursting currents flow,
And shouts attest to Heav'n our joy below.

My crowns of ivy weave, and bring!
    Let Age and Care
    Our banquet share,
And foaming wine-cups sparkles fling,
And kings and beggars swell the festal cry,
And gods for joy on earth forsake the sky!

JUPITER.

Apollo, king of day, respond in song!

APOLLO.

Nay! bend the noble bow!
The graceful quiver take,
Let nerve and muscle grow;
Let strength your courage make;
And thus on form and brow impress
The majesty of manliness.

Then strike the sounding lyre
Till your broad bosoms thrill,
And every pulse is fire,
And deathless grows the will!
Soon Greece will crown you in the game
With laurels of eternal fame.

See round my head these rays!
I who the sun-steeds guide,

The earth, the heaven make blaze,
And life in light provide,
I counsel you to turn from wine,
And in the beams of virtue shine.

JUPITER.

Haste, Beauty's Queen, and try thy tuneful tongue.

VENUS.

Kiss'd by the morn from the foam of the sea
    As I slept on its wave,
Bright Beauty her glory threw over me,
    And I smiled as she gave.

Oh, soon in my breast glow'd love with his fire,
    And quick quiver'd the thrill
That conquers e'en Jove, the all-ruling sire,
    Whom I lead at my will.

Immortals fly forth my train to attend,
    And where brightens my face
Olympus will rush its cycles to spend
    In my beauty's embrace.

JUPITER.

Pure as a summer moon, Diana, sing!

DIANA.

Red midnight comets from their blazing hair
  Will drop down horror on the waken'd earth;
And guilty pleasures, like their fatal glare,
  Start only woe and terror into birth.

'Tis I who rule in peace the virgin-moon,
  Calm type of lawful wedlock's cloudless bliss ;
Oh, at the marriage-altar seek life's boon,
  And find the purest joy in virtue's kiss !

When bow and quiver on my shoulder press,
  As I at morn may brush the sparkling dew,
Oft smiling will I pause your home to bless,
  And richest mercies o'er your life will strow.
        JUPITER.
Quick, merry Cupid, charm us with thy lay !
        CUPID.
    The rose my home,
      My boat a shell,
    O'er earth I roam,
      To cast my spell ;
And when above the clouds I seek to fly,
These radiant wings will bear me to the sky.

    My head beams light,
      My heart thrills love,
    And all things bright
      Wake where I move !
And Heaven bends down to take me with a smile,
Since my small arrows men and gods beguile.

    Make bare thy heart !
      I twang my bow,

Whose pointed dart
Rules all below!
And e'en immortals, when I make them dream,
Too brief will find eternal cycles seem.
   JUPITER.
Great God of battles, peal thy note of war!
   MARS.
Nay! clash the helm and shield!
Brass-armour'd seek the field!
The battle-spear swift hurl,
Where chariots flame and whirl!
Prize on your face the scars
That make you dear to Mars!

Your country served, return
When cease war's fires to burn;
Find deathless your renown,
If Greece shall bind the crown,
And o'er a grateful land
Shall make your statues stand.

Where burns my martial strife,
Seek there the strength of life;
In Heaven's eternal plan
But battle makes the man,
And brightens on the sky
His immortality.

JUPITER.

Valour and Virtue here have won the prize,
In noble strains that please both earth and Heaven.
But see in this world's clay the grace of gods!
Immortal glory shrined in mortal form!
'Tis Hercules, whom painted Pleasure lures,
While smiling Virtue stands, and points to Heaven.

Enter HERCULES, *preceded by* PLEASURE *and* VIRTUE,
who in pantomime enter in opposite directions.
As Passion stirs within her flames, he stops:
But leaves, at Duty's call, the flowers of vice,
And climbs up Virtue's safe but rugged steep,
While over him burst forth celestial strains.
[*Exeunt gods and their attendants amid triumphant music.*

ARISTON.

My friends, ye saw the struggles of my soul
In this bright pageant acted to your gaze;
As ye heard Good and Evil strive in song
So Vice and Virtue battled for my life,
And kept unfix'd my ever-devious will.
None longer linger'd in the revel's blaze,
None oft'ner sipp'd the bloom of honey'd love,
None deeper quaff'd mad joys from each full cup;
But now I feel another destiny;
I'll burst the coils that wind around my soul,

And hurl away this thirsting Cerberus;
In toil, in peril win my fair name back,
To Athens and to Freedom give my life,
And place my image in the Agora
Crown'd with the light of an immortal worth.
Or, should I fall unpitied by the gods,
Since ye, my friends, will never know my grave,
To plant a cypress o'er my exiled dust,
Let memory with a tear blot out my faults!

ACT II.

Scene I.—*A Garden in Athens in view of the sea, and the Acropolis.*

ARISTON.

ATHENA glows on her Acropolis,
And seems to sit a goddess in the sun,
Whose lingering glory turns her form to flame,
And flashes from her spear, while opposite,
The moon is lifting from the sea her face
Round, calm, and full; and near, the star of love
Looks bright as Eos when he eyes the gods,
And from her urn of light drops peace on earth.

Now trembling into heav'n are night's pure lamps
Which burn from age to age, a mystery.
A breath of flowers is in the evening air,
And as the moonbeams slant along the grass
The crimson of the rose is turn'd to gold,
And shadows spread their silence o'er my heart,
While passion's waves sink gentle as this dew,
And reason bathes my soul in calm resolve.
My Ino, come—than yon starr'd blue that round
Enspheres the world, more sweet and pure thy love
Which circles me, and smiles my canopy.

Enter INO.

INO.

Found, truant, found!

ARISTON.

Then for thy pay a kiss!

INO.

Not yet, bad boy! my lips refuse to touch
Till heart and ear are both appeased by thee.

ARISTON.

In me what fault, my girl?

INO.

In thee what fault?
Why, like some school-boy thou art running off,
Or a base fellow who has plunder'd shrines,
Or sold our Athens for a traitor's gold!

ARISTON. 87

Is it a man who will from perils fly?
Stand where thou art and fight! Ariston, stand!
And kisses thou shalt have from lips of mine
More than the rose-leaves, or the smiles of spring,
The notes of birds, and beams of summer moons.

ARISTON.

I'm in no mood for jokes, but sad as sighs!
Before me is a battle long and hard.

INO.

'Tis not in gloom dwells the most fix'd resolve;
The bird that brightest carols o'er its nest
Fights for its brood when ravens croak and fly.
Our smiles more than our tears help on the will,
And the gay laugh gives vigour to the thought;
We mortals, like the earth, must have the sun.

ARISTON.

'Tis so, my girl, and thou, morn's purest ray,
Hast follow'd me as circling light the gods.

INO.

'Twas Heav'n lent me its strength, and whisper'd hope.
Behold yon oak wave o'er the moon its boughs,
While earth is glad to see the child she bears!
This towering tree once in an acorn slept,
Amid decay and circled by the worm;
Yet from that seed this giant majesty.
Thus thou shalt stand aloft, the pride of Greece.

ARISTON.

May all good gods smile on thy prophecy!
E'en more than they are thou and Helia true.
Oh woman's love! it seems a silver'd thread
Bent down by dews, and trembling to the stars
Beneath some fairy's foot, and yet has strength
More than a cable's cords to anchor man
On Virtue's rock when midnight perils roar.

INO.

And yet Ariston from his helpers flies,
Leaves those he loves, and turns their eyes to
    tears,
Tearing the ties which clasp to him their hearts.

ARISTON.

I tell thee, girl, my chain is snapp'd, my foe
Beneath my feet, while stands my will like rock.
Yet still in Athens, 'mid old scenes and friends,
I seem a thing upon the whirlpool's edge,
That circles round, imperill'd, not engulph'd.
As age the cheek, vice wrinkles o'er the soul,
Leaves scars and wounds, and wild and burning
    thoughts,
And voids, and hells behind. Its dead worms gnaw,
While its pale ghosts haunt shivering night and
    day;
Oh, terrible the war! Old habits cling
Like centipedes, and burrow in the flesh,

And taint the blood. They must be weeded out
As interlacing roots that gardens spoil,
And this takes time, and toil, and smiles from gods.
By Heaven's high help I'll make my life anew
'Mid other lands, and when my soul grows strong,
Transfigured in the glory virtue gives,
I'll bring it back to Athens and to thee.
But see, draws near what figure robed in black?

INO.

Thy mother comes!

ARISTON.

Ye gods, can this be she,
With frenzy in her eye, while sadness sits
Pale on her face, the sister of despair?
Yon solemn moon ne'er shone on such a wreck.

[HELIA, *who has been in the distance, approaches,
with* CALOPHOS *behind her unnoticed.*

HELIA.

Oh, he has gone! my son, my son, my son!
Jove bore him off and left me lone and sad;
My poor heart aches till he gives back my boy.
Quick! take its weight away, or I will die!
O moon! on thy bright feet bring down my son,
Or let me go to him from this dark earth.

ARISTON.

Oh! mother, he is here—thy son behold;
Ye gods, have pity on our suffering house!

HELIA (*sings*).
My boy is in the sky,
    Jove took him there;
Lone in this world I cry,
    Despair, despair!

My head is all a-fire,
    My life a sea
Whose billows never tire
    In beating me.

Oh! help me, moon, to thee.
    Quick! I will fly,
My boy, my boy to see,
    Or die—or die.

ARISTON.
Her sorrow breaks my heart! speak, Ino, speak!
Touch her dear hand with thine and lead her off!

INO.
Our Helia, come! do thou with Ino come!

HELIA.
I'll follow thee to Jove, and find my boy.

    [*Exit* HELIA, *led away by* INO, *while*
        CALOPHOS *remains.*

ARISTON.
Oh! Calophos, my path leads o'er her heart!
My absence crazes her! 'tis hard, too hard!

CALOPHOS.

Not this alone, but life itself is hard—
Spun forth by tearless Fates, blind in their work;
Else, dropp'd their threads, would being cease to be.
Through this wild maze the *right* alone can guide.

ARISTON.

The seed I sow'd I reap! Let Vice once grow,
And soon his spoil'd and roguish ways he drops,
To plant down on his slaves a tyrant foot,
Leer out from bloodshot eyes, and cut the flesh,
Till we must fly, and leave his serpent-stings.

CALOPHOS.

Better to fly than feel again his lash.

ARISTON.

My path to virtue winds o'er rocks, along
The chasm's edge, up to the light of Heaven!

CALOPHOS.

Thy lips are guards, not sluices to thy soul;
Hence will I say what else would risk my life.
Who touch her gods will Athens hemlock give,
And yet my son will seek their aid in vain.
There is a Power, of all cause, law, and soul,
Who, like the air embracing round our world,
Wide nature folds with universal life—
And breathes new strength in those who seek the
    right,
And gives new eyes to see the paths of light.

To Him we follow truth, as to the sun
We track the beams which shine in darkest caves,
Or glance their gladness on the poor man's hut,
Or flash in glory round the towers of kings.

ARISTON.

As some sweet spirit of the viewless air
Will toss our words across from hill to hill,
And tell them oft in murmurs dying far,
Long have thy thoughts been echoes in my soul.
These make the groves of Plato musical,
As float celestial notes 'mid earth's wild din,
Soft as the blue through thunder-warring clouds.
Plumes in my breast some new immortal wing
Whose strength will bear me up to that sole Power
Whose guiding voice within thine angel is!
All-arm'd in his bright mail I onward go,
And will for Athens win a conquer'd soul.

Scene II.—*The Court of Persia.*

KING.

GREEKS, I thought, stranger, never bent to
  kings!
Yet thou dost like my eunuch kiss my feet.

ALCANDER.

'Tis best to act as those with whom we live,
And hence, O king, my Persian garb and ways.

KING.

Nay! thou art here to sell thy land for gold,
And hurl thy selfish vengeance back on Greece;
With this thine end to this thine acts conform.
We must each other know without a veil.

ALCANDER.

Athens my life forgot, and banish'd me;
'Tis hence thy royal power I'd plant in Greece,
Which should prefer thy throne to rabble rule.

KING.

Ha! thy pure hope and wish to bless thy state
Which I did deem thee here to sell to me?
Sole is thy aim to save immortal Greece
From tyrant mobs, and not avenge thyself?
Yet say, had not the state thine exile made,
Who more than thee had stood against our arms?
Thy rage has moved to draw us on to Attica,
And with our Persian armies scourge thy land.
A traitor thus will veil his reason's eye
To make his head false as he knows his heart.

ALCANDER.

O King, with insults thou hast met my plans.
Beneath a monarch's robe a Grecian sword
May find a Persian heart.

KING.

'Tis what I thought.
He, selling Greece, will murder him who buys—

Cold as the gold he grasps, or hot his rage
As his own treason serves.

ALCANDER.

O King, I'll go—
No Grecian can endure thy Persian pride.
Before I know this blade will leap to thee.

KING.

Stand, traitor, stand! thou hast no more a will!
Stay there thou must, and do thy proffer'd work.
Move not a space wide as a hair above
Thy false and plotting brain! Around my throne
These glittering spears cry, thirsting for thy blood!
Who barters off the soil that gave him birth
No country has, nor can have friends;
Cursed by the sold, and scorn'd by those who buy
—A mean and loathsome waif upon the world—
The traitor can own nought save his black heart.

ALCANDER.

I will not hear this more, but leave thy court.

KING.

First sign this bond! this bond shall have thy name!

ALCANDER.

I will not sign!

KING.

Sign, Grecian, sign thou shalt!

ALCANDER.

Nay! I will tear the deed, and fling about

Thy throne its rent and scatter'd parts,
And tell thee to thy face I will not sign!

KING.

Brave Greek, we'll see! Guards, draw around
    this wretch!
A hundred naked points flash in thine eyes!
Thy name, quick, down thy name! Come closer,
    slaves!
I see he likes not this bright gleam of steel!
Alcander, 'tis thy bond, drawn by thyself,
Which pledges thee to give o'er Greece to me
When I to thee ten talents pay in gold.
The money there, now make thy pact complete!

ALCANDER.

Forced by thy swords, my name would hold me not.

KING.

That risk I take, 'tis thine to sign the bond.

ALCANDER:

Circled by guards with swords aim'd at my heart,
I write my name, but not my faith I give.

[ALCANDER *signs*.

KING.

Wretch, thou art ours! thy flesh, thy soul are ours!
Go home to Greece! thy deed will follow thee!
Thy name, subscribed by thee, to Athens sent,
Will be our mortgage on thy treacherous neck,
And make thee do, our slave, what thou wilt loathe;

Though far away will move the hand we buy,
To open to our gold the gates of Greece:
Or else will give thy carcass to the mob,
And bring thy brother vultures on thy flesh,
Clouding thy house with an eternal shame.
We cannot love, but we can use thee, Greek!
Thy land we hate where we our armies lost;
Our shatter'd ships yet lie along your shores;
Your temple-shrines our plunder'd trophies deck,
And we will pluck them thence by force or guile.
Thee we despise! thy race for ever hate,
Which, unsubdued, will overthrow all kings,
And give this world to lawless liberty.
We will pour over Greece, weak by thy gifts,
A Persian deluge as when ocean heaves
Itself on shore, or heav'n falls down in floods.
'Tis thus we hold thee in the grasp of fate;
Here Persian spears, and there the Grecian's hate.
    [*Exeunt* KING *and Courtiers.*
ALCANDER.
What line can fathom my deep infamy?
My past, how bright it shows 'mid this lone gloom!
Thine image, Athens, shines most beautiful!
New glory rests on thine Acropolis!
Thine Agora's immortal shapes how fair!
Athena's form towers o'er her Parthenon,
And in his temple Jove majestic sits.

My home seems smiling in the morning light.
Oh, eyes, but weep, till vengeance stops your dew !
The husband loves the bride who charm'd his youth,
Yet, stain'd by her his bed, will choke her cries,
Will rend with steel the form he half adores,
And drop his tears down in the blood he sheds.
Athens, the more I loved, the more I loathe.
On earth for me from hence nor home, nor grave !
For me in eyes no tears, in hands but death ;
Around me roll wild seas of gore and gloom ;
Stung ever onward to the doom I dread—
Afraid to live and more afraid to die.
To my sold soul is left its one dire work—
By Persian swords to draw forth Grecian blood,
And quench the fires of an eternal hate.

ACT III.

Scene I.—*A Grove between the Grecian and the Persian camps.*

ALCANDER.

E Gods, is this my doom ? In Athens I
Dragg'd to the light the crew who
barter'd off
Themselves for bribes—vermin fixed on the state
To suck its blood into their bloated flesh,

And who outhunger the hyena's maw.
I loathed the wretch who sold his soul, then
 fawn'd
For higher bids. Yet now, by Persia bought,
Black spectral fingers reach across the sea,
And with my bond forever lash me on.
O Greece, thy stones cry out against my sin!
Thy waving banners flaunt it to the winds;
The swords of heroes flash it in mine eyes!
The seas in midnight yells fierce roar it forth;
The hills to hills shout my dire treason back,
And the still stars, and the great sun look down
On me in scorn—so paid my pride and rage!

Enter a Persian emissary in a Grecian garb.
Who goes there? stand!
               PERSIAN.
               I come from Persia's king.
               ALCANDER.
Ho! guard! a spy!
               PERSIAN.
               Be still, or thou art dead!
               ALCANDER.
Thou art but mad! So near our camp, my word
Would flash around thy heart ten thousand spears.
               PERSIAN.
Behold this scroll! it is thy pass to me!

ALCANDER.

I know thee not—'tis false!

PERSIAN.

'Tis true, base Greek!

ALCANDER.

What? this to me, and here? I'll have thy life!

PERSIAN.

Put up thy sword, and then this parchment note
Which will ward off from me all Greece, and thee;
Nay! it would stir yon camp of thine to storm,
And bring an army's fury on thy head.

ALCANDER.

Thy riddles cease, and tell what tempts thee here!

PERSIAN.

This is thy bond, which has thy name and seal!
Redeem thy promise to the king of kings!
Take this our gold which here I bring to thee,
Your allies buy, and give Greece to our arms!

ALCANDER.

Slave! hand thou me my bond, or feel my sword!
Here I will tear to shreds my treason's proof,
And give its infamy to scattering winds.
My bond, or death!

PERSIAN.

False Greek, be not too fast!
This is a copy of thy treasonous pact,
And if destroy'd, out from the royal chest

Would leap thy bond, thy ghost that haunts thy
    life,
To scare thy dreams, and hurl all Greece on
    thee.
I dare the blow that on thyself would fall,
And give thy body to the vulture's beak
Cast out on lonely shores, and send thy soul
To shriek and shiver 'mid the mocking shades.
Receive this gold, and with it do our work!

          ALCANDER.

In evil hour, compell'd by flashing swords,
On Persia's hostile soil, I wrote my name.
But slight the deed and dire the penalty!
Ye gods, no place of pardon to my tears?

          PERSIAN.

See thou to that! 'tis ours to claim our due.
But tell the Greeks our weapons forced thy
    name,
And made a coward sell to us their land;
This, more than treason would arouse their rage.

    [ARISTON *and* INO *are seen in the distance.*
Behold thy chief! Ha, now thy colour flies!
One word of mine to him will seal thy doom!
Thy bond fulfil, or die!

          ALCANDER.
                Soft, Persian, soft!
In yonder wood we will talk o'er our plans!
I'll take thy gold; yon boy and Greece I hate!

To ruin them, 'till death I am thy slave.
    [ALCANDER *and the Persian withdraw, while*
    ARISTON *and* INO *enter together.*

INO.

Ere thou left Greece, when training for the games,
What rosy boy did serve thee in thy tent?

ARISTON.

Ino, what dost thou mean? thou knew'st him not.

INO.

With grace he brush'd thy robes and comb'd thy
    curls,
And kept, 'mid summer's heat, thy goblet full
Of water sparkling from the fountain's brim.
Once, when thy chariot with its lion crest
Whirl'd through the dust, and thunder'd by the goal,
While thou like Mars didst stand with guiding
    reins,
And sounding lash, and Greece decreed a crown
Around thy head unknown, thy slave pick'd up
Thy laurell'd circlet which had dropp'd to earth,
And bound it on thy hair.

ARISTON.

              Where wast thou, girl,
To see what I recall, but had forgot?

INO.

In Lydia, too, when thou had'st scaled a wall,
And fell back by a blow, a second slave
Wiped off thy blood, and nursed thee weary weeks.

ARISTON.

Thou art a witch to know and tell such things;
Some god from Asia brought this news to thee!

INO.

Maybe I borrow'd wings from Mercury,
Or Cupid bound his pinions to my feet.
Again, at Tyre, the king, who gave a feast,
Laugh'd at thy fast from wine, and challenged thee,
When thy third slave, who chanced to bear the cup,
Fell down, and spill'd the wine to save thy vow,
But earn'd an oath that made e'en Pluto shake.

ARISTON.

Say, who these slaves? A woman's wit will match
A woman's love, and do what frightens men.

INO.

And when, return'd to Greece, thy grappling ships
Like clasping tigers fought, and stain'd the sea—
Thou gaining fame that makes thee Archon now,
Thy name to Greece unknown, but not to me,
A fourth slave at thy side did watch each blow;
The battle o'er, did spread 'neath stars thy couch,
And when the evening winds touch'd light thy
    cheek
With envied kiss, did fan thee to thy sleep.

ARISTON.

'Twas thou, disguised, who follow'd me to save.
I felt thy sacred presence round my life;

Henceforth I worship thee and not the gods!
My soul subdued from vice now claims thy love.
                        [*They embrace.*
Each here to each we pledge our hearts and lives!
Ye powers who made yon moon, and bent that dome
In starry glory round our circled earth,
Our country watch and girdle with your care,
And on her altar give us strength to die!

             INO.

In this disguise I am Alcander's page!
His daily doves to Persia bear our plans,
Before their bud can blossom into flower.

            ARISTON.

Ye heavens! oh, must a son his father track
Like hounds a fox, and hunt him to his death?

HELIA *enters, still crazed, supposing herself* CERES *in search of* PROSERPINE; *she is crowned with flowers, and carries bearded sheaves.*

             HELIA.

'Twas Pluto stole my dear—she lives in hell.
Oh! weep, with Ceres weep, and weep, and weep!

            ARISTON.

How can I bear a sight which tears my soul?
More worn and crazed than when I left our home.

           HELIA *sings.*

   O king of night, hear thou my cry!
      Give back my child!

A gloom is on the earth and sky
    That makes me wild.

O'er hell's black mouth I scatter flowers
    And fruits and sheaves,
To charm you up, infernal powers,
    Where Ceres grieves.

Send over Styx and up from night,
    My child to-day;
Proserpine, give to the light,
    I pray, I pray!

Enter ALCANDER, *who does not know* ARISTON
as his son.

ALCANDER.

Ha! here my page! Boy, I have sought thee long.
And Helia, thou—who brought thee to the camp?
The slave who let thee loose shall feel my whip.
Both follow me!

HELIA.

Pluto, thou art from hell.
My child, my child! oh, give me back my child!

ALCANDER.

Quick, wife and slave, or I will force you on,

ARISTON.

Alcander, nay! thou shalt not thus be harsh.

ALCANDER.

Shalt, Archon, shalt! thy insults stain my name,
And leave a blot thy blood alone can cleanse.
> [INO *rushes away with* HELIA, *while* ALCANDER *assaults* ARISTON, *and falls insensible after a brief, but as it turns out, not a fatal contest.*

ARISTON.

Oh! blacker grows my life, supernal gods;
A father's blood spots o'er this moonlit earth,
And that red mouth cries out, "thou parricide!"
A sire kill'd by his son, as gives some tree
Upon the mountain's brow a filial limb
Unto the axe that fells its shatter'd trunk;
My hand has pierced the heart that fill'd my veins,
And quench'd in night the soul that lit mine own.
But yet a traitor's that majestic form.
Both shame and grief are in the drops I weep;
The father melts mine eye to tender tears,
The traitor turns the gushing floods to ice.
Thus liberty groans up through death to light.
Here, near my father's flesh, I, freedom's son,
Kneel down, and swear to fight till Greece be free.

SCENE II.—*A tent in the Grecian camp, where the* ARCHON *and* Generals *sit in council.*

ARCHON.

THE trumpet's breath has call'd our council now
    To hear proposals from the Persian king.
Shall Greece at all receive his embassy ?

HEROCLES.

What harm to see a tyrant's messenger ?
Nor fear nor falsehood should impose on Greeks.
I must advise that we should hear the terms;
If they advantage, ours will be the gain;
If they insult, 'twill rouse and weld the states.

CALOPHOS.

I think with Herocles that we should see
And hear our foe in his ambassador;
'Twill wake in us more true and firm resolve.

ARCHON.

Are all agreed that here the Persian speak ?

ALL.

Agreed! agreed!

ARCHON.

    Herald, announce our will !
[*The* Persian ambassador *is introduced.*

ARISTON. 107

AMBASSADOR.

All hail, ye men of Greece, most true and brave !
I have come to you from the king of kings,
Who, like the sun, would shed his beams on all,
And make a world in his bright smile rejoice.

ARCHON.

We have decreed to know thy monarch's wish,
Supposing always nothing will be urged
To hurt the pride, or stain the name of Greece.
This understood, we wait to hear thy words.

AMBASSADOR.

My task is brief; my king's compassion's great;
He fain would spare your blood and give you peace.
Our arms possess your land, our ships your sea;
On yon high mountain-rock amid the clouds
Our monarch sits with Greece beneath his feet;
White gleam his tents where millions flash forth
    fear;
An ocean he, an earthquake to o'erwhelm,
Before destruction sends you terms of grace.
When ye bring earth and water to his throne
He will recall his troops, except a guard,
Impose slight burdens on your tribute state,
And through his satrap rule o'er this your Greece.

ARCHON.

Since we can feel no fear, we ask no grace,
But trust our cause and country to our swords.

With threats of chains Greece would have scorn'd
    thee hence ;
With words of peace she will discuss thy terms.
                  [*Exit* Ambassador.
Let the gods speak before frail men may talk!
But Heaven can counsel earth in such an hour.
Bring in the Priest!

            Enter Priest.

          Most venerable man,
What say the victims and the oracle ?

            PRIEST.

Ye Greeks, I'll tell what I have seen and heard.
White as the snow of Helicon, a lamb
Was on Apollo's marble altar burn'd ;
Soon smoke curl'd o'er the blaze, and through its
    clouds,
As if 'twas born of them, an eagle flew ;
Then flashing down, he sat with balanc'd wing
On Delphi's pinnacle, till circling high
He sunward soar'd in sign of victory.

            ARCHON.

But, Priest, hast thou yet ask'd the Pythoness,
Who from her tripod tells what will the fates ?

            PRIEST.

Before our Delphi's shrine, with streaming locks,
And eyes that seem'd two sparks of lightning-fire,

In whispers first, that rose to thunder-bursts,
'Mid smoke and flame, the frenzied priestess cried:
    When ocean conquers land,
    And the sun leaves the sky,
    Greece Persia will command,
    And Liberty shall die.

    ARCHON.

These words declare to us our victory.
Yet 'tis with us, or chains or liberty:
Calm Prudence sits in council with the brave,
And Courage takes no risk that it may shun,
While in a war of views is wisdom born.
Alcander, tell us what thou dost advise.

    ALCANDER.

My wounds, young chief, may make my cause
    seem weak,
Since blood drain'd from the veins bedims the mind.
Nor are the times propitious to my plea.
Once Greece preferr'd grey hairs to curls of youth,
And scars to boasts, and fame to infamy.
Now heroes hide, and boys to office flash,
While passion rules with wild, impetuous sway.
We seek not laurels, but the good of Greece;
Our aim not crowns for us, but peace for her,
Swarm'd o'er by troops, who, fierce as sea-waves,
    fling
Their Persian fury on our trembling shores.

Can we beat back these floods? When we can hurl
The billows from the sands. Where brave men yield,
Whose blood has flow'd like ours, to save the state,
'Tis no disgrace.   Here weak we are and few,
And there a multitude; our coffers low,
With them exhaustless gold; fierce discord ours,
While to our foes one will.   If we resist,
Chains, fire, and death, but peace if we will yield.
Let Greece repose beneath the Persian throne,
And catch the brightness of an empire's beams!

HEROCLES.

Me have mine ears deceived? or is it so
That Greece has been advised to crouch, a slave?
Shall she bring earth to kings, her past blot out,
And stain the glory which her fathers gave?
Can we not guard what they for us have won?
Nay! what they conquer'd we'll defend till death.
Our chief, 'tis said, is young! at least he's brave,
And bares his arm to strike where age would yield.
Twice in the games he won from all the prize;
By sea and land twice led to victory.
Incarnate Greece lives in his soul, and sheds
Round glory where her hero fights, strewing
With crowns his path to an immortal fame.
Are states disjoin'd? 'Tis Persia's gold divides.
Say, who, Alcander, scatters it conceal'd,
And fills our camp with treasons and with fears?

ARISTON. 111

Wilt *thou* to Persia bear demanded earth?
Thou carry water to the feet of kings?
Wilt *thou* cringe there a slave, where Greece will
    hiss
Thee with eternal scorn? We will not yield!
'Tis ours to fight for Greece, not give her chains,
And lift our race to universal sway.
The gods choose us for freedom's mighty war,
And in their will is an immortal strength.

          CALOPHOS.

Ye Powers above, smile on us while we fight,
Since Heaven helps those to strike who dare the
    blow;
While on our altars fires propitious blaze,
And signs to triumph point and oracles,
The gods will blast us if we think to pause,
And men will call us cowards in their scorn.
Raise, Greeks, the battle-shout of liberty!
When younger, I hurl'd down a rushing foe,
And with his corpses piled our bloody soil.
Again this wrinkled hand shall grasp the spear,
This head shall feel the helm where warriors die.
Let cowards shrink, and traitors counsel peace,
While we the tyrants slay who would chain
    Greece.

          ALCANDER.

Cowards, for me this word? traitors, for me?

Grey hairs a licence claim ; who dares to prove
What Calophos would hint ?
ARCHON.
       Alcander, cease ;
No challenge I permit in such a place.
ALCANDER.
And who, vain youth, art thou ? Thy words beware !
This wound of mine no eyes save ours saw bleed ;
Next, thy rent flesh may let thy life ooze out.
ARCHON.
Speak thus again, and thou shalt be in chains !
ALCANDER.
'Tis chance did make thee rule o'er better men,
While in my veins the oldest blood of Greece.
Who art thou, youth ?
ARCHON.
     Thy son !
ALCANDER.
       'Tis false !
ARISTON.
        'Tis true !
ALCANDER.
That drunkard left my home and died afar.
ARISTON.
Nay ! he return'd disguised, bronzed o'er by war,
And with the lines of vice worn from his face ;
See here the proof, and mark on my right arm—

ARISTON. 113

A word traced there in infancy by thee—
Ariston, read—then on my finger note
The seal of our own house set round in gold.

ALCANDER.

A silly lie which time will tear to shreds;
But if my son, be thine a father's curse!

HEROCLES.

Come, nephew, to my arms—the mist clears off.
We learn why thus our hearts beat warm for thee,
And for her son Greece felt such sympathy.

CALOPHOS.

Ariston, hail! my pupil's voice I know,
And marvel thy disguise could hide thee so.

ALL.

Ariston, hail! All Greece will bid thee, hail!

ARISTON.

Here to this council I unfold my name,
My secret giving to the ear of Greece,
Lest it may perish in the battle-shock.
Wild Pleasure stain'd my life, till Love redeem'd,
And gave me back to live and die for Greece.
Her form I see, as when Athena lifts,
Through some dark cloud o'er the Acropolis,
Her flashing image to the morning sun.
Ye Greeks, a soul resolved is victory.
United stand, and, strengthen'd by the gods,
Hurl Persia from yon hill, and sink her ships

Beneath the weight of the eternal sea!
Only from martyr-drops is Freedom born.
Our deeds will live in song to thrill our sons,
And conquer time by Art's immortal touch,
Till in their splendour coming ages say—
Behold the spot where Greece saved Liberty!

ACT IV.

Scene I.—*Tent of the* King *in the Persian Camp in Greece.*

KING.

HO art thou, Greek?

ALCANDER.

One thou hast seen before
Prays from the ground, O King, and asks thy
    grace.

KING.

Thy face is strange, yet o'er my mem'ry floats
An image from the past that seems like thee.
Ha! now 'tis plain! changed thou art, Alcander!
Thy hair more grey, and much more bent thy form,
And in thy haggard eye a fiercer look.

ALCANDER.

I have perform'd my work, immortal King!

'Tis *that* made white my locks, *that* shook my nerves,
That kindles in mine eye its wilder fire.
Divided Greece, her friends bought off by me,
Cowers at thy feet, and makes my pact complete!

KING.

Thou hast for us been active as the winds,
Fiercer than fire, and tireless as the sea;
Our gold through thee has poison'd Greece
Until her bloated flesh falls from her heart;
Now soon our arms will push her to her grave,
And with her bury freedom from the world.
In her new Archon her sole hope is left.

ALCANDER.

Curse on his upstart head! I'll bring it low.

KING.

To take him off no price too great for us;
Then Persia will chain down the limbs of Greece
Forever fetter'd 'neath my conquering foot.

ALCANDER.

For that I wish not gold, but ask my bond—
To thee a parchment dead, to me a ghost
That haunts my sleep, and stirs up ugly dreams,
And with a leering eye stares o'er my life.
I do demand my bond, naught but my bond,
And for my bond I'll give thy pay in blood.

KING.

Alcander, thou art mad—thy look most wild—

Thy hand with eager clutch clasps round thy
    sword—
I fear thy ways.

            ALCANDER.

            My work has shaken me.
In killing Greece I let her spirit loose
To stand a torturing spectre on my path.
It comes, and glaring cries to have my bond
To silence it—and hence my bond I want,
To hold it thus, and feel it in my palm,
Then give it to the flames, and in its smoke
Roll off each damning token of my crime,
And cleanse my soul, and lay this ghost for me.
My bond, O king, I beg, hand o'er my bond!

            KING.

Thou art most fierce, thy reason is disturb'd
By these remorseful memories of thy life.

            ALCANDER.

Give me my bond, and that my mind will cure!

            KING.

If thou for it the Archon slay, we will;
Persia will bless thee too with rank and gold.

            ALCANDER.

What such poor stuff to me! nought but my bond.
The tiger says what to the silly kid
Who gambols near his lair? A spring, a tooth,
A piercing claw, then a low growl of joy,

While sparks fly out from his too eager eyes,
And quivers with delight his spotted skin;
'Tis nature in the beast, and not his crime.
So I, O king, first wrong'd by Greece, then struck
Down by her chief, by hate and fate urged on,
True to myself will kill thy foe and mine.

KING.

Thy bond is in our chest three leagues away,
But ere this eve thy dove shall bring it thee.

ALCANDER.

O king, enough! I trust to thee my bond.
Send it through air to fly more swift than winds,
And pass on clouds the lightnings as they wink,
Bringing aloft across the night of Heaven
My white-wing'd dove that bears to me my bond,
And back his mate will sail with news to thee,
To redden earth, and turn the skies to blood,
And hurl down Greece to writhe in her own gore,
While thou and I exult to see her die.

SCENE II.—*Tent of* ALCANDER *in the Grecian camp;* INO *disguised as his page.*

ALCANDER.

BOY, see this flame which curls up with a joy,
And seems to say, "Aha, I love my work!"

Give it more oil !
INO.
The lamp will hold no more.
ALCANDER.
Then with the bellows make more fierce the fire !
Breathe on it, Winds, and help me blast my foe !
Note in the flask that small but shining drop,
And tell me, boy, what in its circle sleeps.
INO.
I am, as thou, no alchemist to sway
The shining stars, to bind and loose the winds,
And raise the waves, and bring from herbs their
    powers.
ALCANDER.
In Persia I learn'd that, from an old sage
Who read the heav'ns e'en as the books he wrote,
And moved to life and death the elements.
His hair was snow, but then his eye was flame,
And seem'd to look dilate across the grave
Till to its glance all hidden things stood plain.
He taught me how to make yon glittering drop
Where I see life and death lie side by side.
There Persia's fate and there the fate of Greece ;
Oh ! more to me that drop than Asian gems !
It makes me free !—see if the dove has come.
INO (*standing at the tent door*).
The moon is up, just lifting from the sea ;

And quick she climbs above the summer mists,
Flinging across the waves her track of beams;
But not a speck is on the brilliant sky.

ALCANDER.

Thou liest, slave! Look out with sharper gaze!
I cannot leave my fire e'en for my bond.
What dove is missing now from out our cote?

INO.

He is a Syrian dove, and of the flock
I noted him the king. No arrow wing'd
With beams from bright Apollo's bow will fly
More swift than he will dart, and reach thy tent.

ALCANDER.

A noble bird, whose breast with silver'd hues
Gleams like yon moon—his pointed pinions made
To outspeed winds, and round his neck my fate.

INO.

Why is it, master, that our Grecian doves
Do fly but to and from the Persian camp?

ALCANDER.

What means that, boy? Stand here before this flame!
A guileless soul is beaming from thy face;
Thy glance is clear, and I do wish no words.
My trust is in thine eyes more than thy lips:
If false, thy heart shall quiver on this steel.

INO.

How thou dost scare thy slave! E'en in thy dreams
Thy teeth will gnash—thy words freeze o'er my
    blood.

ALCANDER.

Tell on thy life what thou hast heard me say!

INO.

Last night when cried the guard his last lone hour,
Our lamp was low; while I toss'd on my bed,
In the dim ray, I saw thee work thy face
And grind thy jaw; thine eyes stood from thy head,
Thy hands were clasp'd, and round thy limbs did
    twist,
As from thy breast oppress'd came stifled moans.

ALCANDER.

Boy, 'twas a dream, and yet its torment dire;
The moon pass'd o'er the sun fring'd round with
    flame,
And darkness sat on earth with twilight mix'd;
The stars next turn'd to blood, and whirling fell
Caught in a comet's hair, while all the sky
Seem'd like my shrivelling bond; birds sought
    their boughs,
And beasts cower'd to their dens as if the sun
    were dead,
And owls and bats flew over stalking shapes;
Then on a cloud Athena shook her snakes,

And seized my hair to fling me from the sky,
While monsters swarm'd o'er Greece to tear my
    flesh;
But, boy, enough! Look for the bird once more.

INO.

I see it cross the moon! it comes! it comes!
I hear its wings! It circles o'er our tent!

ALCANDER.

Be quick, my slave! I cannot leave my fire;
Take from the dove my bond and bring it here.
    [INO *goes to the dove, and untying the bond flings
    it behind the tent to* ARISTON, *and brings to*
    ALCANDER *a blank piece of paper.*

INO.

My master, all is right! Here is thy bond!
I knew our Syrian dove was true of wing.

ALCANDER.

Thanks to the gods! I'm safe if Persia fails,
And Grecian eyes should search her conquer'd
    camp.
I'll read my bond, then give it to the flames
To roll away my infamy in air.
            [*He opens the paper in the lamp-light.*
'Tis blank! I'm duped! the villain king has lied!
The Fates are at my throat to clutch and kill!
Again the ghost of Greece glares down on me!
Slave, art thou false? find thou my bond, or die!

INO.

Master, oh blame me not! that from the dove
Tied on his faithful neck I brought to thee.

ALCANDER.

Out, slave! bring forth the lamp, and search with
me!

[*They leave the tent, and while looking around,*
Ariston *enters from behind with soldiers.*

ARISTON.

We seize Alcander in the name of Greece.

ALCANDER.

Back, I say! back, nor dare to touch my flesh!
Base slave who sold my blood, I hurl thee down.

[Alcander *flings* Ino *on the ground.*

Come on! come on! I chains and Greece defy!
Mean upstart, I will never yield to thee!
Ye stand and fear, and own my better blood!
Those fetters shall not bind Alcander's arms!

[*After a short but severe struggle* Alcander *is
bound and forced away.*

ARISTON.

My Ino sinks, struck by my father's hand!
Oh live, my love, or I will die with thee!
Now from this stream I'll bathe her cold, white
brow!
Bring back, ye glistening drops, her life to me!
Ye pulses, start, and give this cheek its bloom!

Ino! Ino! 'tis thy Ariston calls,
And bids thy spirit come to its fair clay!
See me these eyes, and speak these marbled lips
Which here I kiss, and rise this form whose grace
Doth robe a shape sent down to me from Heav'n!
Oh, he who hides in earth her whom he loves
Entombs his life, and makes this world a grave!
She breathes! she stirs! I thank the listening
    Powers!

Scene III.—*A Dungeon.* Alcander *in chains.*

ALCANDER.

E Gods! my brain is fire! my heart is
    stone!
    Wild horrors throng these walls and shake
    my soul.
Grim, goblin shapes come creeping o'er my gloom;
Old warriors seam'd with wounds, meek matrons
    slain,
And mangled babes with their reproachful eyes,
Look down on me, while spirits shriek around,
And furies hurl red torches through the air.
'Tis Greece with corpses piled lies on my breast
With an eternal weight—the cause, my bond
Which sign'd me o'er to hell to do its work—

My everlasting lash to whip me on.
The traitor sells himself, and buys such joy!

Enter ARISTON *bearing a lamp.*

Out of my sight! this is the worst of all!
The deadly snake more welcome here than thee.

ARISTON.

Father, forgive! 'tis Fate decrees our doom.

ALCANDER.

Forgive! that word and thee I would blot out.
Look on my chain! who bound it on my wrist?
Who scarr'd my flesh, and sent me to this gloom,
And on my forehead fix'd a traitor's mark?
Ariston, *thou!*

ARISTON.

I can undo it all,
And set thee free. We fear not Persian arms,
But Persian gold, and know not whom to trust.
Greece sits on battle's edge in dismal doubt;
Chief chief suspects, and soldier soldier fears.
Show who is bought, and Greece forgets the past,
And gives its glory to our clouded house.

ALCANDER.

Nay, let her die! my hand would hurl the torch
Of blasting war, not quench for her its flames.
Let Persia plant her throne, and rule our mobs!

ARISTON.

I only seek in thine the good of Greece,
And beg thee save her from a tyrant's chain.

ALCANDER.

Should I confess, thou'dst be a traitor's son,
Tainted thy blood, and cursed our house and name;
Thy welfare and mine own would seal my lips.

ARISTON.

Thou dost relent! thy heart melts o'er thy son!
Down at thy feet he prays for perill'd Greece!

ALCANDER.

Relent! with blows, if thou this chain take off;
Relent! as tigers do when mouth'd in blood;
Relent! as furies when they blast with flames.
My dungeon's gloom leave thou in peace to me!
Thy quest insulting doth assume my guilt.

ARISTON.

Too much we know—thy bond is in my hand,
Borne by thy dove from Persia's camp to me.

ALCANDER.

My bond a proof with thee is death to me!
Each tie is snapp'd that binds to this grim earth.
Thou shalt live spotted with thy father's blood;
This poison on my lip compell'd by thee!
It turns my veins to fire, and burns my brain:
Thy work, my son, who brought me here to
    die:

These pangs from thee; I gasp to curse thy soul,
And leave my heir his heritage in hate.   [*Dies.*

ARISTON.

Oh! this indeed is death! His touch like stone
Chills on my flesh, and round the air seems ice!
Stiff as the chains that bind are now his limbs!
In this dim flame his eyes stare on me hate,
And on his lip stands yet his lingering curse;
His soul stays here to blast me ere it leave.
Oh! through these clouds, Athena, shine o'er
    Greece,
And from thy locks shake ruin on our foes,
Crowning our brows with thine immortal beams!

ACT V.

SCENE I.—*A Grove before a temple of Minerva.*

ARISTON.

AM once more a Greek, and joyance
    leaps
On through my blood fresh as this
    morning air,
Whose bosom throbs to fill the world with life;
Our manhood grows but in the light of joy.

INO.

A Greek's a bird whose pulse has thrills of glee,

ARISTON.

And sings each day as if no next would be.

ARISTON.

Ino, I've had enough to sober me:
A father's death, a mother's wreck, the wars
Of struggling Greece!

INO.

        Once more the shadow comes.

ARISTON.

And then the battle to subdue myself!

INO.

Enough! I'll run away, or else will stop
With kisses thy sad lips. Go seek the crown
In games, or chase along the hills the boar,
Or smile to see thee on the mimic stage!
Woman loves sunshine in the eye of man,
Has faith in him who in himself has hope,
And strength to screen her from the tempest's force.

ARISTON.

Ino, well said! Buy Plato's cloak and gown,
And teach to listening Greece the ways of life.

INO.

Before I join with thee, thou tyro, tell,
Tell, was it I or not who track'd thy step,
And follow'd like a ghost to watch thy ways,
Or others paid by me to bring report.

ARISTON.

Graceful and trim, 'twas thou, my pretty boy.

INO.

I say not it was I, but this I think
Her air was manly if her cheek was smooth;
She e'en thyself did rival in the camp,
And took the soldiers' hearts, who stroked her curls,
While, swaggering, she did joke more than they all.

ARISTON.

My Ino, stop—I cannot think 'twas thou.

INO.

Strange if that boy had won thy place and name;
Immortal he in marbles made by Greece!

ARISTON.

Say thou no more! Draw o'er those days a veil!

INO.

I have no blush for what I did for thee;
The love that urged the deed preserved my sex.
Look on my cheek! there sits a woman's bloom.
Gaze in mine eye! there beams a woman's light.
Search through my heart! there lives a woman's
 love.

ARISTON.

High o'er Athena's shrine thy page's dress
A gift to Heav'n shall hang, dear next thyself.

INO.

But did I say 'twas I who follow'd thee?
I'll take it back—it was some moonstruck dunce—
Or else my shade that left myself in Greece

To glide abroad, and keep a watch o'er thee.
But cease such words! Behold thy mother there,
Who seems some form in which the gods breathe
    grace,
That they may see a matron's dignity!

HELIA.

I've pass'd through Hades, Styx and Pluto seen;
All earth I've search'd, and walk'd on ocean's
    floor;
Olympus climb'd, and stepp'd up into Heav'n—

INO.

Oh, look, our Helia, here!

HELIA.

                    That voice I know,
And it is like the murmur of the sea
So sad in shells and moans along the shore.

INO.

I Ino am!

HELIA.

            That name comes from the past,
And lifts a cloud away from memory.

ARISTON.

Mother, I am thy son!

HELIA.

                How dear that tone,
And how familiar too! My boy's sweet voice,
When prattling as a child, more manly grown!

K

ARISTON.

Ariston I! Oh, touch my face, and gaze
Into mine eye, and know I am thy son!

HELIA.

The marbles in the Agora like thee!

INO.

These were his images placed there by Greece!
This is thy son, thy true, thine only son!

HELIA.

Then let me feel thy hand and stroke thy cheek;
My fingers tell my brain more than mine eyes.
Thou art the same who in the statues stands!
My gloom is gone! I see a light like day!
Ariston thou, and Ino by thy side,
I know you both and clasp you to my heart.

[*All embrace.*

The world is fill'd with joy too great for life!
Athena, from thy temple look and hear
Me vow myself to be forever thine!
Upon thine altars grateful lambs shall burn,
While heav'n and earth glow o'er with light and
   song!

*Enter girls and boys, garlanded, who dance singing
around* HELIA, INO, *and* ARISTON.

Hail, son of Greece! who like Mars in the morning,
   Through red clouds of battle gleam'd fierce on
      our sight;

Oh, now over Heaven thy glory adorning
  Will send round the earth the sweet beams of
    thy light.

Hail, son of Greece! when the Persian's mad
    minions
  Bore torch and the chain to the land that we
    love,
Thou seemedst an eagle hurl'd swift on his pinions,
  And swoop'd from his mountain-nest, scaring
    the dove.

Hail, son of Greece! bright around thee thy glory
  Like that on the heads of our heroes doth shine!
ARISTON shall live in song and in story;
  Immortal with Greece he his name shall en-
    twine.

Scene II.—*A porch before the Temple of Jupiter in a grove.*

HEROCLES.

HOW bright Apollos drives his steeds to-day
That earth and sky may smile in light
    on Greece!
The air breathes joyous life, the sea-waves dance;
Sweet flowers from brilliant leaves give grateful
    scents;
The very birds seem glad, and azure-crown'd
Hymettus in his love stands kissing heaven.

CALOPHOS.

Some power unknown has thus hurl'd off our foe,
Who more than Jove deserves a temple here;
To him be thanks who sits throned o'er our gods.
One day the Persian's arms are girdling Greece,
The next, our land beholds his ghastly dead,
While o'er the sea are strewn his shatter'd ships.

ARISTON.

But terrible the price of liberty!
Brave Aristippus, Philippon the true,
Iolo, with the shades! With batter'd helm
And shield, and spear-pierced through the neck,
    the first

I saw beneath a Median's foot pour out his life.
The next, on snorting horse whose eye shot fire,
Was hurl'd amid the foe, where Syrian darts
That flew in clouds did hide my friend from view.
Iolo, oh! ye gods, how hard his fate!
I saw him stagger, fighting as he fell,
Gash'd o'er by wounds, until a Persian cleft
His gory head, and hurl'd it high through air.
May such a sight salute no more mine eyes!
CALOPHOS.
Well, now 'tis o'er, the dead beyond recall,
And ours it is in joy to give our thanks.
HEROCLES.
Thy youth, Ariston, show'd in one mad charge,
Which hurl'd a handful on a Persian horde,
While up a hill was thy wild murderous rush.
ARISTON.
The only test of war is victory,
Which oft gives crowns where we deserve an axe.
Not in our flesh our hope, but in our *souls!*
Army to army match'd, and ship to ship
We were mere madmen beating ocean back.
Despair that wins, must be in *act* despair;
The *onward* snowflakes make the avalanche;
The *onward* flames will mountains wrap in fire.
HEROCLES.
Nephew, I own that thy defence is good.

But see! there come the spoils of Jupiter!

ARISTON.

Gods! let these trophies stir the heart of Greece,
And loose her lip to shake the dome of Heav'n!

Enter People *and* Soldiers *bearing the
spoils of battle.*

HEROCLES.

See there a tatter'd Syrian banner float
Stiff with its splendid blazonry of gold!
One Spartan snatch'd it from a hundred guards.
There come the quiver of a Scythian chief,
An Arab's bow, and his fire-breathing horse!
That Persian shield round as its flashing sun;
And from some royal brow the Median helm!
Yon crown's bright gem burns like an eye of Mars.
Pile upon pile, and snatch'd from land and sea,
An empire's spoils our noble triumph show.

ARISTON.

Good Calophos, the trophies are prepared.
Herald, peal o'er the grove a signal blast!
Let all Greece bow while earth gives thanks to
  Heav'n!   [*All kneel.*

CALOPHOS.

Olympian Jove, thy majesty we own;
Thine are the skies, and thine this lower world,
Whose eye beholds, whose power encircles all,

ARISTON.

While nations can but rise and fall in thee.
From thy high throne of clouds regard our Greece,
Accept her thanks for thundering on her foes,
And to her soil eternal Freedom grant!
The spoils receive we place before thee now,
And smile propitious while we utter praise.
[*All arise.*

HEROCLES.

Now, Calophos, thy gracious task discharge!

CALOPHOS.

To her whose vigilance was bless'd to Greece
Has been decreed this dove of Persian gold;
The Agora to Ino votes the gift.

ARISTON.

Our thanks to Athens for her grateful love!

CALOPHOS.

In this gemm'd picture sleeps a youth on flowers,
Beneath whom roars a torrent dash'd o'er rocks,
While sits a mother near her dreaming son;
Above I read these words in letter'd gold—
"Helia's maternal love has Athens saved."

ARISTON.

My tears dropp'd on the gift evince my heart.

CALOPHOS.

Ariston, taken from our battle-spoils
I hold a crown for thine own brow decreed;
Bright-blazon'd on its jewell'd rim I read—

" All Greece Ariston calls deliverer ! "
[ARISTON *kneels, is crowned by* CALOPHOS *amid the shouts of the People, and then, rising, speaks.*

ARISTON.

My Calophos, first honour to the gods
From whose immortal wings drop victory:
As their own gift we take the praise of Greece.
Yet 'mid these shouts, and circled with this crown,
I here do blush that I can boast no scar,
While I see those who from grim battle pluck'd,
Not graceful wreaths, but victory with wounds.
The private soldier bears the brunt of war,
And wins the garland his commander wears.
There stands a man whose arm is on the field,
And at his side is one who left his blood.
That soldier's eyes, pierced through, see not this
    pomp,
While he, a sailor, on a grappling ship
Lost both his hands, which, dropping, tinged the
    sea.
Yon brave man's breast was fill'd with Scythian
    darts,
And from this vet'ran's flesh I pluck'd a spear.
Go where the jackals yell and vultures fly,
To find their dust who saved, and smile o'er
    Greece !
Where battle laid them low, carved from their spoils,

To them immortal monuments shall rise;
While on our coins, and chanted in our songs,
Their names shall teach our sons to die for Greece.
Eternal Freedom lives in martyr deeds.

THE JEWISH CAPTIVES.

THE JEWISH CAPTIVES.

ACT I.

SCENE I.—*A Private Garden in Babylon.*

ELI.

Y gentle Eva, tune thy harp, and sing
Till these blind eyes see old Judea's hills,
And feel the captive's comfort of a tear.

EVA.

Oh! father, in these strings still sleeps a spell
To charm away each sorrow from thy soul,
But my sad touch can wake no music now;
When circling hawks cast shadows on its nest,
The bird to Heav'n trills not its morning joy.

ELI.

I love to hear the songs of thy young life;
More sad my gloom, more deep my solitude,
Without thy harp and lip to give me cheer.

142 THE JEWISH CAPTIVES.

EVA.

'Tis soul, and not the sound, melts grief away;
Song loves liberty as the birds love light,
And when the cage is still the grove bursts forth.
Just as the heart is bound the lip is cold.
But, father, on yon willow let me hang
My silent harp, and tell to thee my dream,
And when my cloud has pass'd my song may flow.

ELI.

My Eva, take my hand, and lead me where
Oft with thy mother I have stood and gazed;
Her image there, she whispers through my gloom.

[EVA *guides* ELI *to the willow, against which she places her harp, when they sit under the shade on a grassy bank*].

EVA.

Father, would thou couldst see yon golden sky
Where paints the sun his crimson on the clouds;
The light and shadow chasing o'er the grass;
These oaks that join their patriarchal limbs
Across yon stream, bright-flashing when 'tis seen,
Yet murmuring music though its way be hid,
And teaching us, if dark our path, to sing!

ELI.

No light for these poor eyes shut up in gloom,
But morn and noon and night to me the same.
When blindness came, at first my heart grew hard;

Oh! now within a sun, no more to set,
Outshining him who fills the earth and sky.
Quick, Eva, tell thy dream!

    EVA.

    My mother's voice
Comes back like angel-whispers in the eve,
As she once told the story of thy home
That smiled 'mid bloom above the temple hill.
My memory hears around Jerusalem
The tramp of men, the thunder-bursting yells,
And blows upon the gates—along the streets
The clang of hoofs and the wild noise of war,
While flames I see that from the temple roll,
And glare o'er heav'n, as when my mother spoke.
I feel again the pain of your long march,
To reach a captive's place where false gods rule.
Father, in dreams last night I saw your dear
Old home wrapp'd round with fire, and forth I rose,
It seem'd, out from the flames, when, as I flew,
Some monster clasp'd me shrieking round my
    waist
And bore me high o'er clouds, until we dropp'd
Within a palace-hall of Babylon.

    ELI.

My Eva, cease this tale which pains my ear;
Some midnight magic has call'd forth bad dreams,
Or fever in thy brain wakes shapes of fire;

Or evil angels have lurk'd o'er thy couch.
Not from the Source of Good wild phantoms come.

EVA.

Father, this dream leaves on my breast a weight
Like some cold stone, while in my head whirls fire.

Enter ABNER *and* ONO.

ELI.

Ha! lads, I know your steps, and my old ear
Grows quick to hear how goes the city's siege.

ABNER.

Thy prophets, father, have deceived us Jews
With words as false and frail as painted mists;
Thy priests must now the light from Heav'n bring
    back
By death-drops from the heart of some poor lamb
Whose pangs should blast, not bless its murderers.

ELI.

My son, speak not in scorn of things now hid
Behind the cloud that veils thy Maker's plans!

ABNER.

Jehovah sleeps while Baal crowns his sons;
They sit in purple and we weep in dust.

ONO.

The captive's wail shall turn to triumph song
With Him who rules a cycle is a day;
We wait, or trust, or strike as He may say.

ABNER.

The two-leaved gates defy the Persian's blows:
Her walls like mountains stand round Babylon.
Here fields and gardens bloom, and Plenty smiles
With stores piled up to Heav'n, while gaunt
    without
The troops of Cyrus stalk like skeletons,
And boys and women mock them from the towers.
Their very banners hang with sickly droop
As if they shrank away from vigorous winds.
Factions divide, the hungry nations jar;
And men thy prophets said would break our chains
Will see their armies soon like clouds dissolve.

ONO.

Cousin, despair and youth should never wed,
More than the frost should marry with the fire;
Let Faith and Hope smile angels on our path,
And they will nerve our hearts for victory.

ELI.

Yes! through my gloom a cloud of glory gleams
Bright o'er thy rebuilt towers, Jerusalem!
Belshazzar's gorgeous piles shall shake and fall!
O'er them shall darkness brood, and hoot the owl,
And the lean fox lone o'er their ruins look,
While Zion's hill stands in eternal light!

[*Here* EVA, *who has retired behind the trees, takes
    her harp and sings.*

EVA.

Brother, trust! 'tis God hath spoken!
   Israel soon will cease to roam!
Brother, trust! each battle-token
   Soon will show us near our home!

God has call'd—the nations hearken;
   Round our walls their banners fly;
Over earth their armies darken;
   Send their shouts into the sky.

Hark! on stones a hoof is ringing!
   Arms on arms! I hear the clash!
Up to Heav'n the flames are springing!
   Wild o'er Babylon their flash!

There I see a monarch lying!
   Blazes round a banquet's light!
Blood is on him, gasping, dying—
   Torn his crown and gone his might!

One king lies there grim and gory,
   Crown'd his victor I behold!
Over Zion bursts new glory!
   Stands her temple as of old!

SCENE II.—*A room in the house of* ELI *overlooking a garden.*

ONO.

CAPTIVITY makes gloom, and tries our
    hearts;
Yet morn shall come from night with sun
    and song.

ABNER.

But ere the dawn my youth in me is dead:—
My life a void, and yet an agony.
I hate myself, and oft my Maker hate,
And feel that I would hurl Him from His throne.
'Twas He, not I, who made me thus for pain.
Who forges chains, and wakes the pangs of war,
And stains with blood a world He strews with
    graves,
Forcing from man this universal wail?
I, a mortal, would relieve the woe,
While He who can, you say, nor hears, nor helps.

ONO.

Thy youth is aged, thy hair is early grey
With bitterness, which, not thy years, makes old.
What robs the eye of fire, and blood of joy
With nature wars—of evil root ill fruit.

ABNER.

Ono, we have enough to craze our souls.

See on the throne of Babylon a fool,
Yet flashing in his splendour like a god,
Whose nod can make the streets run with our blood,
And hang a dangling Jew from every tree,
Then cut us down, and turn us o'er to dogs!
Yes! Eli is a slave—Belshazzar, king;
Virtue in chains and tyranny in gold.
A life like ours can't find a grave too soon.

ONO.

Belshazzar is a captive to his lusts,
And Eli monarch by his goodness crown'd,
In wisdom rich and throned in hearts he loves.

ABNER.

I'm tired of this old tale, and life's dull pain;
Weary with heart-beats and the load I bear.
Along our streets the boys shout out, "A Jew!"
The simpering girl will smirk and whisper, "Jew!"
The beggar sneering cries, " A Jew! A Jew!"
The slave will mutter as he mocks us, "Jew!"
Could God thus curse his sons, and bless their foes?
His throne seems void, His universe a blank.

ONO.

Thy thoughts in words but make the pang more sharp;
The stem that feels the knife gives brightest bloom,

Fields torn with ploughs wave with the richest
    gold,
And loudest tempests leave the sweetest calm.

                    ABNER.
Ono, mere words; the thorn will pierce thee, too;
There is in each some spot most sensitive
Which will resent the steel.   Cut *other* flesh,
The man is still; touch *that*, and he will smite.

                    ONO.
There is from Heaven a help to those who trust.
   ABNER (*pointing through a window to* EVA *leading*
            ELI *through the garden*).
Behold a sight that should draw tears from
    rocks,
And ask if it will bring one drop from Heaven?
See Innocence lead Age along yon walk!
'Tis Beauty helping Wisdom on in love.
Think of that angel in Belshazzar's arms!
Ha! thou dost start! the point is in *thine* heart;
The pallor of thy cheek shows me thy faith.

                    ONO.
Jehovah, save her from the monster's clasp!
Ne'er let him blast the bloom of my sweet
    flower!

                    ABNER.
Pray not, but strike—strike to the tyrant's heart:
Thy sword will save her better than thy trust.

ONO.

There is a time to suffer and to slay;
When Heaven will have us smite it shows the way.

Enter GORGIAS *and* ATYS, *Officers of* BELSHAZZAR.

ABNER.

Whence do ye come, and what your errand here?
Who hear our words by stealth must feel our swords.

ATYS.

Be calm, brave Jew, and hold us as thy friends!
We too have felt at last the tyrant's heel;
Goaded too deep the ass himself rebels.

ABNER.

Made near by common wrongs, we welcome you!
My hope revives! A cloud lifts from our race;
I feel the blush of shame for my despair.
Light hence with us—with Babylon the gloom!

ONO.

But tell us, princes, why ye seek us here,
And we will swear with you to right our wrongs.

GORGIAS.

Both crime and folly shake Belshazzar's throne;
Within, oppression drains the empire's veins,
Without, 'tis destiny has arm'd our foe.
The gorgeous pile nods o'er the brink of fate,
And needed but one touch to dash it down.

Atys, recount the tyrant's last mad blow!
My gasping son would choke my words with groans.

ATYS.

The park ye know, in which, high o'er our walls,
The terraced garden mounts amid the clouds;
Well, near its base of bloom, on flying steeds
We chased a boar; Belshazzar led the way.
In his swift flight the tusky monster turn'd;
Belshazzar hurl'd his spear with girlish arm,
And headlong sprawl'd on earth beneath his horse
Close to the glaring boar, which rush'd on him,
When, quick, Ozona's sword was in the beast,
That sent its spouting blood to stain the king;
And then, ye gods, the tyrant struck the lad,
Who fell down dead beneath his father's feet!

ONO.

That blow sounds out the knell of Babylon,
Beats down her walls and shakes her shatter'd
    throne,
The Persian crowns, and sends the Jew forth free
To build again Jerusalem, our joy!

ABNER.

Princes, we will dare all to burst our chains!
But tell us how that we can give you aid.

ATYS.

Cyrus, we hear, grows weary with the siege,
His troops desert, his stores and hopes are low;

Fame says ye have a scroll that gives his name,
Foretelling, ages since, his victory;
To him we'd bear the book, and nerve his heart.

Enter ELI led by EVA.

ABNER.

My father see—this blind old man who comes!
That book he deems the gift of Heav'n to us;
Nor could a kingdom buy it from his grasp.

ELI.

The winds have borne strange voices to mine ear,
And in their breath I scent some coming joy.

ONO.

Here, uncle, stand two princes next the throne,
Who, outraged by the king, his ruin plan.

ELI.

Hail, blest of Heav'n! Our deliverers, hail!
O'er these blind eyes hope streams prophetic light.
But what your plans?

ONO.

Our Holy book
They would to Cyrus bear, and show his name,
And where 'tis said he'll pass the two-leaved gates.

ELI.

Never shall Gentile hands the Word profane
If Israel linger here to die in chains!
But ye, my children, ye shall take the scroll!

Oh! Heav'n guard well the gift bestow'd on me!
[ELI *is led by* EVA *to a golden chest, and unlocking
it, he lifts out a large parchment.*
Accept the trust, and unto blood defend,
And swear that ye will bring it to these hands!
Ono, swear!

ONO.

I swear!

ELI.

Abner, thou!

ABNER.

I swear!

ELI.

Can ye unbar your gates, and scale your walls
To Cyrus reach?

GORGIAS.

A passage deep beneath
Our streets will lead us, devious, to the plain,
And near the Persian camp, while here its keys—
My family trust!

ELI.

Go, with my blessing, go!
Jehovah guide you through the cavern'd earth!
Jehovah move the Persian's royal soul!
These feet shall touch the land I may not see!
These ears shall hear the song on Zion's hill
When to the skies our temple lifts its head!

GORGIAS.

But now, good Jew, we must pierce to thy heart,
To save from worse than death one thou dost love.

ELI.

This breast has felt the storm so fierce and oft
That, like a trunk scarr'd on the mountain's top,
It dreads no blast that roars to make it fall.

GORGIAS.

Thy daughter, Jew, thy daughter should retire,
That we may speak to thee.

EVA.

                Heav'n in my dreams
Has show'd it me, when I, borne in mid-air,
Was by a monster clasp'd—Belshazzar, he.

ATYS.

Too true, too true! He marks thee for his own!
The tiger's spring less sure than his foul lust,
Whose snares would lure thy beauty to his arms.

EVA.

Father, speak not, nor roll thine eyes in pain!
Nor, Abner, grasp thy sword, and glare so fierce!
My Ono, stand not like despair in stone!
Now in this hour which tests my faith in Heav'n
I feel within the might of virtue lives
To breathe a conquering vigour through my soul;
And oh! a shield so strong is over me
That its bright face will dazzle my foul foe.

No stain shall ever mar my virgin bloom,
But from Belshazzar I will come as pure
As the fresh leaf of my own morning rose,
Which knows no kiss save of the dew and breeze.
Omnipotent the might of virtue's power;
A true pure heart is an immortal flower.

SCENE III.—*A Piazza on the Hanging Garden.*

BELSHAZZAR.

WHIM, Atossa, call it what thou wilt,
Me like a bubble lures, and I do chase
The glittering thing, since 'tis my destiny.

ATOSSA.

My royal insect, say, o'er what flower next,
To sip its sweets, wilt wave thy brilliant wings?
Soon from this world its honey suck'd, the gods
Must make a better one; and then for thee,
When each is stale, a brighter than the old,
And thus for ever on.

BELSHAZZAR.

Immortal jest!
Wit, mirth, wine, women, feasts and priests in turn
Have to my hours tied wings and painted them,
Till they would fly like clouds to leave me blank.

ATOSSA.

Thou king of kings, what phantom lures thee now,
Since thou dost look like some sick lad in love?

BELSHAZZAR.

Atossa, laugh, and I'll endure thy jests,
For thou art but myself in woman's form;
Nor polish'd steel thine image gives more true
Than thou art mirror'd in thy brother's soul.

ATOSSA.

While Cyrus girdles round thy throne with war,
Would I could lead thee off from virgins' breasts
To stand with men in battle for thy crown!

BELSHAZZAR.

War is the work of fools — to wear a helm
And plume, and live shut up in brass,
And thirst, and starve, and stagger 'neath your toil,
Then hack and kill to pile o'er plains with men
Whose flesh shall fatten dogs, and for your pay
A rabble's shout, *this* glory's vaunted prize
Which Cyrus loves, and can have for himself
While last my stores, and walls resist his blows.
With wine and love I still will brighten life,
My crown esteem just for the joys it brings,
And when these die, the bauble give my foe.

ATOSSA.

A boy art thou, Belshazzar, not a king.
But now the secret that doth load thy heart!

THE JEWISH CAPTIVES. 157

BELSHAZZAR.

Sister, I love, in truth at last I love ;
The snarer snared—and more, I would be loved,
And if not loved I'm lost, and at an end
This insect life, stifled by its gay threads.

ATOSSA.

Nay, brother, nay ! the royal whim will pass,
And thou wilt lie, flower-crown'd, on beauty's
    breast,
Or sit gay-garlanded where flows the wine,
And song floats out with harp and dulcimer.

BELSHAZZAR.

A rose of Sharon in my palace blooms
More dear to me than crowns, and on my breast
I'll wear my Jewish flower, or die accursed.
The soul was in me once to make a man,
But I was born a king—*that* blasted it.
'Tis love must turn my blight to bloom, and fit
Me for my diadem ; or, oh ! ye flowers,
Ye trees on terraces piled into heav'n
By my great ancestor—ye walls he rear'd
O'ertopping clouds—thou watch-tower lone of
    stars—
Ye palaces and trophied monuments,
Built from a plunder'd world to blaze our fame,
But stain'd with tears and blood, link'd with you
    all

By fate, must I too fall, and share your curse?
Death's pulse beats in my life as oft I hear
Wild shrieks drown mirth beneath my battlements.
A sword waves o'er yon towers, and round my crown
A serpent coils, and sins of ages flame,
Until I seem like that last mountain-pine
Whose shroud of fire is the whole forest's blaze.

ATOSSA.

What means thy mood and tones of prophecy?
This feather see, whose history I will tell!
As I stood here to view the Persian camp
Whose arms and banners glitter'd in the sun,
On a white horse rode Cyrus grandly forth,
And while I gazed, a brilliant bird flash'd by,
On which down from the clouds an eagle swoop'd,
With beak to bear aloft the crested thing,
When circling to my feet this feather fell.

BELSHAZZAR.

Give me the painted plume—sign of myself,
The sport of winds—to place it in my crown
Above mine empire's gems, a type of fate!
But hark, a hell-bird comes to croak my doom!

ATOSSA.

I will retire, nor hear our mother rage.

                        [ATOSSA *exit.*

BELSHAZZAR.

I will not fear, but pay her with her own;
This plume stuck in my crown will madden her.

Enter NITOCRIS *and* MADETES.

NITOCRIS.

A feather in thy cap—fit diadem
For thee, thou king of mighty Babylon!

BELSHAZZAR.

'Tis this I wear which to my nature suits
That I did suck out from those queenly breasts.

NITOCRIS.

Nay! from thy nurse thy folly flow'd to thee;
Nor blood nor milk of mine made such a son.
But play no more the boy! that plume take off!
Put on thy helm, and grasp thy sword and shield!
Where harps and moonlit pipes now soothe thy
    sense
Let trumpets peal the battle-blast of war!
Thy robes of silk exchange for links of steel!
The smiles of women for fierce blows with men!
Thy feasts for fasts, thy shame for victory!

BELSHAZZAR.

Cease, mother, cease!

NITOCRIS.

        Arm, Belshazzar, arm!
Down from this height your leaguer'd city view,

Her glory circled by eternal walls!
Earth's crown is now for thee to hold or lose.
Where stood thine ancestor with kingly eye
To see arise his work, there wilt thou stand
To see it fall? the towers he built, wilt thou
Look hence on them while Persians hurl them
    down?
Say, came from me, my son, a soul like that?

          BELSHAZZAR.

I beg thee, stop!

          NITOCRIS.

    And I do beg thee *fight!*

          MADETES.

Low on the earth I crawl and grasp thy knees;
Thy faithful eunuch prays thee save thy crown.

          BELSHAZZAR.

'Tis ye, if Cyrus wear it, are the cause.

          NITOCRIS.

This is thy folly now to madness turn'd!
Give me thy diadem! Thine armour fit
Around thy mother's form! Above her brow
Thy helm should wave its plume! Her hand will
    hurl
For thee amid the battle's shock thy spear;
And when our foe shall fly it shall be told
Along our streets, and thunder'd up to clouds,
That thine old mother saved for thee thy realm,

While thou, bedeck'd with flowers, and lull'd by
    lutes,
Didst on thy couches feast with concubines.
BELSHAZZAR.
Insult me not—thy king as well as son!
I blame thee for a mother's too fond love.
My youth was flush'd with noble dreams of war,
The trumpet stirr'd my pulses into fire,
Until I sought the field to be a king.
Thy coward love did hedge me in with boys,
Where Pleasure tied me with her silken cords,
And took the manhood from my pamper'd soul;
But who has power to win will keep his crown;
Brave men will scorn weak kings, and hurl them
    down.
Thus those to empire born dig their own graves,
While enterprise takes strength from wave and
    storm,
To crush voluptuous heirs and moutn their thrones.
I see the truth too late to shun my doom;
Eternal Fate mine empire sinks in gloom.

ACT II.

Scene I.—*The Camp of* Cyrus *before Babylon.*

CYRUS.

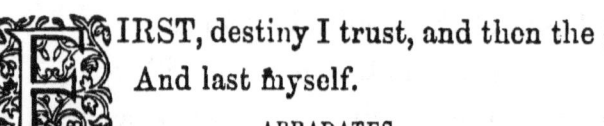IRST, destiny I trust, and then the gods,
And last myself.

ABRADATES.

Forgive our doubt, O king,
And that we tire of this dull, dragging siege;
Despair looks from the faces of our men.
Better our armies move by thy command,
Than troops of thine steal home like fugitives.

GYGES.

'Tis two years since 'mid shouts thy hand did give
Our banner to the winds before these walls.
While we are lank, flush'd Plenty smiles within,
And those unshaken towers laugh at our rams.

ABRADATES.

The clash of arms 'mid battle's breath of fire
And tug of death, we love—not idle war.

CYRUS.

True soldiers wait, or fight as gods decree,
Whose smile alone points on to victory.

ABRADATES.

Never since first my wheels in battle rush'd
Have whirl'd my steeds my chariot from the foe:
Yet now I'd hear the trumpet sound retreat.

CYRUS.

Such blast, my friend, will never please thine ear.
With beauty robed, as Panthea smiles on thee,
So Babylon, my queen, still lures me on
To bind the crown of Persia on her brow.

ABRADATES.

Fast as my steeds, whose fire is from the sun,
Can draw my grateful wheels, I'll go with thee.

CYRUS.

Despairing Crœsus, too, I tell thee now,
So sure as thou wast pluck'd from cruel fire,
I'll mount yon tower whose head strikes on the stars,
And fling from thence my flag o'er Babylon.

CRŒSUS.

O king, I yield to thee, and doubt no more;
What Cyrus wills in war is destiny.
But give, we beg, the reasons of thy faith.

CYRUS.

True men have one prime object of their lives
Which Heaven helps on, and all below are steps
Like climbing stairs that circle round a tower
To gain its top, and give us prospect wide.
Up to one grand event which caps the whole

Mounts every step of my predestin'd past.
My Persian birth, the breath of liberty,
The discipline that nerved both flesh and soul,
And throned as lord of all my will:
The royal splendours then of Media's court,
Nay! e'en my grandsire's polish'd luxury;
Each after-move on this chess-board of life,
Where Fate ranged men around me as their king,
But bore me on to fix my banner here.
My dreams in youth were flush'd with Babylon,
And when they troop'd like gorgeous clouds along
She was the sun that lit their splendours up.
My manhood now stands center'd in her light;
Take her away, my path is all a gloom,
My life a chaos of discordant plans;
With her in view, one blaze of victory!
As day's consenting beams meet in the sun,
So all my being ends in Babylon.

Enter GORGIAS *and* ATYS *with* ABNER *and* ONO,
guarded by Persian Soldiers.

Say, who are these with beards and hair forlorn,
And hunger lean, and garments soil'd by earth?
In these I seem to see our way made plain.

OFFICER.

We heard, O king! beneath the ground a cry
Suppress'd and faint, as shook the soil with blows;

)ades, and digg'd down to a stone,
ɔw'd these weak and groping men,
)y the light we led to thee.

                  [Officer *retires*.

GORGIAS.

ias so begrimed and vile
annot discern his face?

CYRUS.

ls thee now—I know thee well.
ince I met in Lydia once,
d save me from a lion's mouth.

GORGIAS.

not say that but for me
abylon could ne'er be thine.

CYRUS.

ιou wilt not—my life thou saved,
worn in token of my thanks
rest with rampant paws.
st, my friend, and not my foe.

GORGIAS.

ny brother's son, with me,
ng Jews, here pledge thee swords
ιls.
ll kneel, and kiss the hand of CYRUS.

CYRUS.

ːriends! Long may I call you such!
brought you here in such a plight!

GORGIAS.

I seek my vengeance for my first-born's blood—
My noble boy struck by the tyrant dead;
Atys joins with me to avenge his kin;
These Jews would from their country burst her chains.

CYRUS.

Thanks to the gods, your guides to bring you here!

GORGIAS.

We heard, O king, thy hopes had sunk, and soon
Thy baffled army would to Persia turn.
These Jews have brought that which will nerve thy soul,
Inspire thy men, and give thee Babylon.

CYRUS.

I see, good Jews, ye bear an ancient scroll
Which seems to wake strange throbbings in my breast.

ABNER.

Within our temple, 'neath a cloud of light,
An ark of gold once held this sacred book
Which the Jehovah wrote on Sinai's side,
And gave to Moses that our race might guard.
When blazed Chaldean flames about the place,
A priest, my sire, to save this holy scroll,
Rush'd through the fire, and caught it to his breast,

But came out blind who brought to us such light.
The sightless man has kept his treasure hid,
Till now he sends us here to show thy name
Writ down before thy birth, and for this hour,
To gird thee on with strength to Babylon.
Here read that thou shalt pass the gates of brass,
Chaldea's treasures seize, and set us free.
We hail thee, Cyrus, our predestin'd king!
ALL.
We hail thee Lord of lords, and King of kings!
> [ABNER *and* ONO *kneel before* CYRUS *with the open scroll.*

CYRUS.
I read in Jewish characters my name,
And my prophetic work by Heav'n foretold;
A flash from destiny thus lights me on
To drain the river, and creep 'neath the walls.
I saw in dreams one standing on a hill
Against the sky, and circled round with rays,
While glitter'd in his hand for me a crown.
All things do point us on to Babylon.

Scene II.—*A room in the palace of Babylon.*

Eva (*alone*).

I SHALL not fall, since o'er me is His shield,
Who doth make pure the virgin lily's bloom,
And the bright stars, and the sweet breath of Heav'n.
We bruise the rose to get its scented drop,
And out from me will trial fragrance fling.
'Tis Battle by its blows keeps Valour strong,
While Pleasure, flush and full, smiles Virtue down,
And bribes the guards about her citadel.
In hue and shape here beauty lives, here music breathes,
And odours charm, till I swim in such dreams
As fancy paints in evening's magic tints;
The senses these may please, not buy the heart.
True woman's love cannot be had for crowns;
Be he a slave or king, it seeks a *man*;
And ere it find it is a humming bird
To glance from flower to flower, but, nested once,
A nightingale that thrills out constant songs.

Enter Belshazzar *in his crown and royal robes.*

BELSHAZZAR.

A witch by Jewish law is judg'd to flames,

And she who scorches me should burn herself.
EVA.
Why seek the fire that never goes to thee?
Thy parrot singed avoids the harmful blaze.
BELSHAZZAR.
Thou art the lamp, and I the moth that flies
To fall upon the bosom of the flame.
EVA.
Nay! be no more an insect but a king;
Seek thou to wed from thine own royal rank,
One who will bind thy monarch-limbs in steel,
And urge thee drive the Persian from thy walls.
BELSHAZZAR.
Girl, I'm a fool to beg a captive's love
When I could force thee to my clasping arms,
Where beauty o'er my realm but pants to lie.
Yet 'tis my wish to hear thee say "I love,"
And see thee at my side a willing wife.
I would not break the stem that holds the flower,
Or spoil by force the bloom that is its pride;
Give me thy heart and I will be a man.
EVA.
I cannot, king, since 'tis another's right!
His, sign'd and seal'd by an eternal pledge,
Which, broke by me, would worthless make
    myself—
A ring whose holes do show the jewel gone.

BELSHAZZAR.

To bless cannot be wrong, and thy pure love
Would make my nature new, my passions tame,
Start in my breast the pulses of true life,
Enplume my brow, and case my limbs in mail,
Till I by valour earn'd the crown I wear.

EVA.

What I have sign'd away I cannot give.
Could I pierce him I love with mortal pain,
His vows betray, and trample on his heart,
And blast his faith in me till I would live
No more his star, but in his soul a blot?
Thou art too noble, king, to ask me this.

BELSHAZZAR.

Proud slave, I'll plead no more, nor let thee fling
My empire's crown away like some worn toy.
The monarch of the world kneels down to thee,
And wilt thou say another has thy love,
Spurning thy king as if he bark'd, thy cur?
My nod an empire shakes, and it would bring
Ten thousand here whose beauty rivals thine.

EVA.

Belshazzar, let them come where I will not.
Say, can thy sceptre force the rose to bloom,
And fill the morning with its scented breath?
A king may crush the flower, not make it live,
And take from hearts their blood, but not their love.

BELSHAZZAR.

Slave, I can pluck the honey from thy flesh,
And leave a stain to make thy lover loathe—
Make thee in thine own eyes a thing despoil'd.

EVA.

Thou canst not, king! I in thy palace stand,
Thy guards around with points of flashing steel,
An empire thine, yet in Jehovah safe.
Old Eli's prayer is stronger than thy throne,
And holds o'er me Omnipotence, my shield.

BELSHAZZAR.

Girl, that there is in thee I may not touch :
Some spell doth keep thee stronger than my lust,
And better guards thee than would warrior's mail.
Repulsed by thee I rush on to my doom ;
The curse of ages thunders in my breast,
And round my brow fall shadows from my fate.

[*Exit* BELSHAZZAR.

EVA.

Belshazzar, sad thy doom to be a king !
Oh ! had thy gifts been nursed in poverty,
Made hard by toil, and large by enterprise,
Thy crown by its own weight had kept thy brow ;
Ancestral power has sunk thee to a boy,
Inviting daring to thy tottering realm,
Where Cyrus soon will build a vigorous state.
I pity thee ! am thankless for myself.

Thou who dost still the storm and lay the wave,
And teach all evil to work out Thy will,
I bless Thee for Thy help in peril's hour!
When hung a cloud to flash on me its curse,
And blast my life with one eternal pang,
Thy breath dispell'd, and I stood crown'd with light.

ACT III.

Scene I.—*A Room in the Palace of Babylon.*

BELSHAZZAR.

TEN wild beasts caged and fighting for
    their food,
Less mad than priests who quarrel o'er
    their gods;
I'll prove that ye love me e'en more than them.
Speak, Smerdis, first, and answer what I urge.

SMERDIS.

I kiss thy royal feet, and pray the sun
To dart his radiant wisdom through thy mind.

BELSHAZZAR.

Priest! I will put thy faith to my own test.
This image see of wood! Is that thy god?

SMERDIS.

Dazzling and vast, our Baal is yon sun,
Whose universal light gives life to all:
Yet in this statue doth his glory shrine.

BELSHAZZAR.

Thy god, the king of heaven, can guard himself,
And blast the arm that hence would hurl him down!

SMERDIS.

Far as his splendid beams can reach his power,
And in their light all wisdom stands reveal'd.

BELSHAZZAR.

Now let thy god have care! I strike his head!
There see it roll, and rumble on the floor!
This trunk is left, which I do thus push o'er,
And order to the fire and roast thy god.
First on his neck I place my kingly foot;
A mortal here insults immortal power,
Nor feels its vengeance thunder on his brow.
Renounce thy lies, or else renounce thine ears!

SMERDIS.

O'er me, O King, thy wisdom hath prevail'd.
If Baal will not care, then care not I;
Let thou mine ears be mine, my god a lie!

BELSHAZZAR.

Smerdis, enough! I see how deep's thy faith!
Far better, my Madetes, is our creed!

MADETES.

From light and darkness I think all doth spring.
To shrines and statues I will nothing bring;
On altars I good flesh will never throw,
Since from his god the priest will steal I know.
The earth our temple is, hung round by air,
Yon heav'n its dome, the sun, its lamp, shines there;
Our world eternal in itself doth stand,
Nor skies, nor stars need a supporting hand;
From nothing we do come, to nothing go,
And hence short lives should gild with pleasure's
    glow.
Each flower we want, we pluck, nor ask a god
What we shall think or feel beneath the sod.

BELSHAZZAR.

To me most loyal truth, who will not own,
On earth, in heav'n, a power above my throne.
Since I myself of all am only king,
Hence to the winds all fears and cares I fling;
Let Cyrus gather glory from his toil,
'Tis pleasure's bloom I snatch, and make my spoil!

MADETES.

Majestic lord of all, stand firm by this—
Make this world sure, and thou art sure of bliss.

BELSHAZZAR.

Old Eli, thy calm face doth trouble me;
Down at my feet, blind Jew, and own me god!

THE JEWISH CAPTIVES.   175

ELI.

O king, I worship Him who spread the skies,
The earth holds up, and lights the sun and stars,
And kindles in each soul its spark of life.

BELSHAZZAR.

Stop, Jew! beware! An empire's weight on thee
Shall crush thy faith and bend thee to my will.

ELI.

Tear out this tongue, O king, and rend these limbs,
Torture my flesh with flames, my soul send forth
From this poor body scarr'd or burn'd by thee!
Like Baal's image thus far I am thine;
There stops thy power! Beyond, I am mine own,
Nor can thy royal might my spirit force;
Jehovah first and last I will adore.
Thy records read! Learn how the Hebrew youth
Walk'd harmless in the fire that burn'd their
        bonds;
An angel's hand was Daniel's shield from death!

BELSHAZZAR.

The lies of priests but by their dupes believed!
Where is thy temple, Jew? thine altars where?
And where Jehovah's prophets and his kings?
Thy God, omnipotent, deserts His own,
And leaves His city to the flames of foes!
See in thyself how silly is thy trust!
Blind, and captive, Eli, curse thy God!

ELI.

'Tis for his sin, O king, that Israel serves;
This wreathes our yoke, and robes our lives in
    gloom;
When flow true tears then grace to us will flow;
Our chains will then drop off, our temple rise,
While we on our own soil will kneel and praise.
Firm as Himself Jehovah's word shall stand!

BELSHAZZAR.

Ha, Jew! A thought flies flashing o'er my brain!
I'll test thy God! Down 'neath our Baal's tower,
Thy sacred things which in thy temple stood,
Begirt by lamps and priests, now guarded lie;
Thy God I'll dare, and bring them up from thence,
And they shall glitter on my festal board.
Better serve me than rust beneath the ground!
Thy God's own lamps shall shine, and see me drink
From His blest goblets our bright Baal's wine:
And mark it, Jew, and grave it on thy soul,
Then tell it to thy God, and ask His help,
Which thou wilt need—hear, Jew, whom I do hate
Next to thy God—thou from Jehovah's cups
Shalt drink with me, or I will torture thee,
Then fling thee o'er our walls to Persian dogs,
And see how well thy God will guard His Priest.

Scene II.—*The Tower of Belus.*

BELSHAZZAR.

LOATHE to live, and yet dread more to die.
To hide the past I'd blot the future out,
But from the void of nothingness shrink back.
I'm like some mount whose ice hides eating flames.
This sightless Jew a devil stirs in me
Who wakes above an Eye that looks me through.
One shatter'd god I've turn'd by fire to smoke,
And here will prove Jehovah too a lie.

Enter MADETES.

Madetes, brave old man, in time for work!

MADETES.

O King, I go alone—risk not thy life!

BELSHAZZAR.

By Baal, no! down I will walk with thee
If shakes the earth; and Heav'n shall fall on me
I'll crown my feast, and dare what Cyrus dreads;
He offers to the gods whom I defy.

MADETES.

Maybe this thundering storm should make thee pause.

BELSHAZZAR.

Dost thou draw back? Madetes proved a boy,

And in his lingering breast a fear of gods!
Does this tower shake, and nod against the winds?
Do yon skies roar, and quiver on the clouds
Quick-flashing fires? Groans this world now in
    death?
'Tis in the din of such tempestuous war
I will descend, and beard this Jewish god.

  [*They pass down a dark stairway, leading through
    a subterranean aisle, to the place of the sacred
    things.*

MADETES.

A dim and lonely place! Yet will we on!
The storm's mad noise here soon will die away.

BELSHAZZAR.

Madetes, stop! that song most wild and strange!

MADETES.

I hear no sound save the far tempest's voice,
Whose roarings sink to whispers in this gloom.

FIRST SPIRIT.

From realms where ne'er can flash the light
I come, I come who make the night,
And soon, Belshazzar, soon I'll roll
Eternal gloom around thy soul.

BELSHAZZAR.

My pulse is calm! no drop is on my brow!
And yet I swear I heard the words as plain
As if they murmur'd from Atossa's lip.

SECOND SPIRIT.

The Spirit of sound is o'er thee, King,
Thro' earth, and thro' heav'n whose thunders ring;
By this loud peal I do warn thee now
To fly, or feel my blight on thy brow.

BELSHAZZAR.

'Tis not my terror shapes such words in air,
As I to mortal ears may ne'er repeat.

MADETES.

Nay! here all's still, howe'er the tower may rock.

BELSHAZZAR.

For me, not thee these warning angels sing,
And hence the aisles of sound in thee are shut.

THIRD SPIRIT.

I flashing come, the Soul of fire;
I hurl the lightnings in mine ire,
    To blast along the sea
    And on the land to kill;
    So terrible their glee,
    So fierce to do my will.
Back, false Belshazzar, whence thou came!
On thee I'll dart my zig-zag flame.

BELSHAZZAR.

All elements combine—earth, air, and fire—
And Hades rises here to drive me back.

MADETES.

Nay, oh my king, 'tis but thy fancy hears;

Since round us broods the silence of the night,
And scarce I note our foot-fall on the stones.

FOURTH SPIRIT.

I'm the Spirit of Power, the Spirit of Power,
To hurl down the ship, and to shake down the tower;
'Tis grim Death at my side that rideth with me,
As I rush o'er the land and dash o'er the sea.
I'm the Spirit of Power, the Spirit of Power,
And, Belshazzar, go back, or short is thine hour!

BELSHAZZAR.

Could I be turn'd, these words would drive me off.
But see the gleam of yonder glittering lamps
Which kindle in my breast resolve so strong,
Jehovah's breath can never put it out!

FIFTH SPIRIT.

Thy blood, Belshazzar, from me flows,
Who won the crown that round thee glows;
Thy kingdom stands built by my hand,
Thy scepter sways by my command.
Now by the flesh and by the bones
Of all our kings beneath these stones;
Now by their souls which death holds here,
And all their hope and all their fear,
I warn thee, son, away! away!
And seek the realms where shines the day;
Else on thy brow Fate writes thy doom,
And soon will hurl thee to thy tomb,

While on thy name and line a blot,
And on thy soul eternal spot.
Thy foe upon thy throne shall sit,
Then Ruin o'er his empire flit;
The bat shall fly, and hoot the owl,
The fox shall lurk, the wolf shall prowl,
While Babylon beneath the ground
Lies ages hid in dust, to be by strangers found.

BELSHAZZAR.

Thou father of our line, dost thou speak this?
I hurl thy curses back upon thy head,
And still will on where tempts our bright'ning
    prize!

MADETES.

The priests asleep, behold the sacred things
Most brilliant in the blaze of watchful lamps!
These holy curs snore well beneath the ground!
Pierce thou that Jew, O King, and I will this!
    [BELSHAZZAR *and* MADETES *each kills a priest.*

BELSHAZZAR.

No thunders burst, nor lightnings may flash here;
These vessels in our grasp, we'll dare their God!

MADETES.

The dastard priests I'll strip, and in their robes
Will tie our prize and take it up to light.

BELSHAZZAR.

Madetes, well! I'll help thee bear thy load

Nor let Jehovah pluck it from my arms!
A watchful God when we can slay his priests,
Their garments take, and rob him of his gold!
He sleeps, or feels that I'm the stronger king.
His arm is powerless, or he'd crush me now;
Immortal glory lights Belshazzar's brow.

ACT IV.

SCENE.—*The Banqueting-hall of the Palace;* BELSHAZZAR *in purple robes, crowned and sceptered on his throne, before him a table with a goblet of wine on the mercy-seat of the Jewish temple.* ELI *on one side, and* SAMMO, *an ape, opposite, dressed as High Priest,* SMERDIS *and* MADETES *sitting just below* BELSHAZZAR; *the Lords of the Empire at a table extending around the room, and near its middle a pile of the Jewish sacred utensils, while a hundred spearmen stand in a square around* ELI.

BELSHAZZAR.

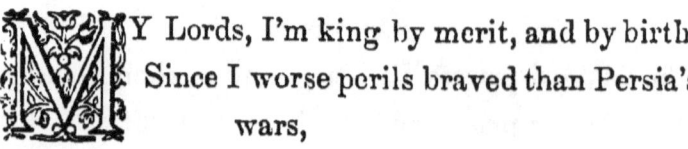Y Lords, I'm king by merit, and by birth,
Since I worse perils braved than Persia's wars,
And ventured down where Cyrus dared not go.
These splendid gifts I from Jehovah took,

While rock'd our frighten'd tower up into heav'n,
And thunder, storm, and fire 'mid cavern'd gloom,
With warning spirits, strove to keep me back.
Hence I sit god of Earth! take Heav'n who will!

MADETES.

From Jewish cups we pour to thee our wine!

SMERDIS.

Once priest of sun and moon, I worship thee!

COURTIERS.

Hail! thou Belshazzar, hail! our king and god.

BELSHAZZAR.

Am I not better than a power unseen—
A phantom born of fear and hence despised —
My crown can flash its glory in your eyes;
My scepter ye behold grasp'd by my hand,
As I impurpled sit on earth my throne;
A god in flesh, and not in wood or stone.

ALL.

We worship thee, Belshazzar, only thee!

BELSHAZZAR.

And Sammo there, with grave and mitred brow,
In sacerdotal robes, I name my priest!
Gone now my faith in gods, I turn to brutes,
And feel a glowing brotherhood with them.
Sammo has eyes, and what have we men more?
He hears, feels, smells, and tastes, and so do we.
He knows, and loves, and hates just like ourselves,

In blood, and bone, and food, and flesh the same,
While death will turn us into common dust.
See Sammo as he drains Jehovah's cup,
And my true priest, pours out his wine to me!
Eli, my ape more loyal is than thee.

ELI.

Blasted the hand and lip that mock my God!

BELSHAZZAR.

Ha! thou dost curse me, Jew, and curse my priest!
Yet better he than thee! The ape has eyes,
While blind the Jew! The ape doth love his king;
The Jew doth hate! The ape will reverence
Where the Jew blasphemes! Blest by me the ape:
Thou, Jew, my slave, and old and sightless too!
Forsake thy god who leaves thee thus to me:
To Sammo I more kind than he to thee.

ELI.

Clouds on His throne, above yet all is bright;
Him I adore Who is Eternal Light.

BELSHAZZAR.

Around me here my splendid empire sits,
And in this blaze of lamps, Jew, thou shalt kneel
Before my lords, and own Belshazzar god.
Draw closer, guards! Point at his breast your
    spears!

ELI.

Thee I defy, but welcome give thy steel!

BELSHAZZAR.

Thy lips have fix'd thy doom! Be ready, slaves!
Each aim his weapon true, and to the heart!—
But stay your spears! What writes on yonder
    wall?
A phantom-hand moves there beneath a cloud,
And traces mystic characters of fire!
It tells my tottering empire's fate and mine!
Jehovah is the god, and this his hand!
Apostate Priests, explain those words, or die!
Ye tremble and are dumb! Guards, pierce them
    through!
No mercy beg! Your agonies are vain!
If I am damn'd, I thus make sure your doom!
Jew, thou art free, and by Jehovah saved!
Throned, crown'd, and scepter'd, here I'll meet my
    fate.

ELI.

Lo! Daniel comes! He'll read these words for
    thee—
May be through penitence may give thee life!

Enter DANIEL, *who kneels before the throne, and then
    slowly rises.*

BELSHAZZAR.

By Heav'n's kind guidance brought now near this
    place,
Thou, prophet of Jehovah, art my hope!

What mean those blazing words that blast my
    sight?

DANIEL.

These vessels sacred to our temple's use
By thee profaned have waked Jehovah's wrath.
Weigh'd in His balance thou art wanting found:
The Medes and Persians will thine empire take.

BELSHAZZAR.

Jew, on thy brow plays Heav'n's own holy fire,
And I thy words believe that seal my fate.
About thy neck I hang this chain of gold,
And robe thee with the scarlet badge of kings.
Yea! all too late I offer to thy God,
Before whose eye we monarchs are but dust!
There bursts the storm! I hear the clash of arms!
Lo! over Babylon the glare of flames!
I'll die a king and near mine empire's throne!

Enter GORGIAS, ATYS, ABNER, *and* ONO, *with Persian
soldiers, who kill* BELSHAZZAR *bravely fighting.*

GORGIAS.

Ye Princes, and ye Lords of Babylon!
The troops of Cyrus o'er your palace swarm,
Your city hold, your gates and towers possess.
See there your king discrown'd, and in his blood—
Last of a race who steep'd a world in tears!
Heavy on him the sins of ages press!

These sacred gifts, profaned, his madness show;
Yon Jew, and mitred ape his blasphemy.
Your plunder'd wealth, your persons scarr'd by
    wounds,
Your state by taxes drain'd, and eunuchs robb'd,
Your murder'd sons, your wives and daughters
    stain'd,
Have doom'd this bloated empire to its death.
Both Heav'n and Earth combine to end such rule,
And hide in night the star of Babylon,
Which, o'er the throne of Cyrus now will rise,
And like a sun will bless a subject world.

ACT V.

SCENE I.—*A Hall in the Palace of Babylon*—CYRUS *in purple robes, crowned and sceptered on his throne, surrounded by courtiers.*

            CYRUS.

PRINCES, and Lords, our throne made
    strong and sure,
We will inquire what touches our wide
    realm.
Regions remote by highways now drawn near,

Make Babylon our mighty empire's heart,
That pulses out its life to each far part.
Tell, Atys, how our posts our kingdoms join!
ATYS.
So swift from town to town, and state to state
Our riders rushing fly, that in ten days,
As borne on winds, our capital has news
From India's plains of fire, and Scythia's snows.
And Tigris with the Ganges seems to talk,
And North to South, and East to West are bound.
Our doves bear over heav'n, as wing'd by it,
What speediest we would hear, until our realm
Is like a room where whispering sounds grow loud.
CYRUS.
Atys, thou hast done well, and proved me wise.
A monarch's glory is to choose fit men,
Each for his sphere, and then his empire is
One body moved, and order'd by one soul.
My Gorgias, are our Satrapies well fill'd?
Our rulers should be mirrors of ourselves,
As we do image forth the King of day,
Who sends his blest and bounteous beams on all.
GORGIAS.
Each satrap to thine empire's farthest bound
By me is chosen from the land he rules,
That knit to it by birth and blood and speech,
His acts may be with knowledge, and in love.

States to thy throne are held like anchor'd ships,
Whose cables keep them from the tossing sea.

CYRUS.

Most cheering this ! Till **Peace** war's wounds has
heal'd,
And from her horn pour'd plenty o'er our realm,
Let Egypt doze, and dream along her Nile !
When ready, we leviathan will wake,
And lay his carcass rotting on his shores.

GORGIAS.

A noble Jew would seek thy presence, King,
If thee it please, and plead his nation's cause.

CYRUS.

Let him draw near : I owe his race a debt.
In a dark hour one brought a light to me
Whose ray led on to this Chaldean throne,
And stream'd around my brow immortal beams.

Enter ELI, *led by* ABNER *and* ONO.

That form I know, and that most princely face !
I've seen it in my boyhood's morning dreams
On Persia's hills, and in the Median groves,
Till it seems link'd to all my life by fate.
Old Jew, my father's self not better known
Than thou, who waved me on to Babylon
Like some bright angel standing in the sun.
My life's long dream, I clasp thee to my heart !

CYRUS *embraces* ELI.

These younger Jews I know, and welcome them!
Ye bore the Holy Book which brought me here!
Ask, Eli, what thou wilt, and it is thine,
E'en to the jewels sparkling in my crown.

ELI.

Most gracious King, from Heav'n thy matchless
    gifts!
Jehovah watch'd thy youth, thy manhood led,
And throned thee here to give us liberty.
Jerusalem is low, tears on her cheeks,
And sorrow in her heart, widow'd and lone,
And sitting in the dust weigh'd down by chains.
Our fetters break, and send us to our land
That we may build on Zion's holy hill
Our temple high, crown'd with the light of Heav'n!

CYRUS.

Good Jew, 'tis done! My scribes, record my will!
Gold thou shalt have, and make thy city shine
In glory worthy of King David's line.

ELI.

Thanks to thee, King, and to Jehovah, praise!
My eyes see not, but oh! my heart can feel,
And I can drop a tear to show my joy.
An old man's blessing rest on thee and thine;
Thine empire live while sun and moon may
    shine!

CYRUS.

Ye Princes and ye Lords of Babylon,
But in eternal right can stand our throne,
By Love and Justice clasp'd, while Heav'n smiles
    down!
If kings oppress, the people will rebel,
And hurl at last base tyrants from their seats.
Rulers who grind the poor to pamper lust
Like monstrous wild beasts should be chased to
    death.
Good Jew, I've done what Justice claim'd as due ;
Jehovah guard my realm, and Israel bless!

SCENE II.—*A Cloister of the Temple of Jerusalem, which alone had survived the fire of the Chaldeans.*

ELI.

O keen my sense, that when across the moon
    The evening bat on leaden wing may flit,
    I feel its shadow moving o'er mine eyes ;
And I can hear the velvet-footed fox
Who lurks and looks along the broken wall.
Such added pain and power my blindness gives,
Since one sense lost, the rest its life receive.
Oh, in this cloister'd spot, saved from the fire
If blacken'd by its breath, I'd rather be

Than on the throne of purple Babylon.
Thank Heav'n I have no mem'ries here from sight!
My last glance saw our temple robed in flames,
Each dying glory heighten'd in their blaze;
Nor did I see Belshazzar's face, or land,
And bless the night that veil'd them from mine
    eyes.
Oh here, Jehovah, let thy servant die—
From here mine eyes be open'd on thy face!
And here my flesh lie down to take its rest,
Then borne out hence to our dear mountain-tomb!
But I hear Abner's step upon the stones!

Enter ABNER.

What news, my son, from our long-building wall?
I have not heard since morn the trowel's clink.
Instead, there rose one burst of sudden joy,
That spent itself, and deeper silence left.

ABNER.

Father, the wall is done—our city saved,
And we have raised an altar on this hill
To have at morn and eve the sacrifice.
Our shouts thou heardst, that burst from heart to
    lip,
While the calm skies look'd down and smiled their
    love.

ELI.

To Israel's God the praise! His name I bless!
He led us through our night to glory's dawn!
This day's immortal—tell me more of it!

ABNER.

The wall was built, except a corner'd part,
When up on us Samaria hurl'd a troop
With one last desp'rate shock to stop our work;
Like some mad stream that foams o'er mountain
    rocks
Our Ono charged the foe, their leader struck,
Who headless from his horse fell to the earth,
And then the Jews, made bold, rush'd on with
    shouts,
Flash'd high their swords, and drove the robbers
    back,
While all the hill was ghastly with their dead.
I then call'd round our men to end their work,
And ere the sun could mark one lingering hour,
So hot their zeal, they shouted it was done.

ELI.

Oh, I can see Jerusalem again
Climb down these vales, and gleam along our
    hills,
And in her midst our pillar'd temple rise!
Here, son, the mantle of my priesthood take,
And, mitred, slay for me the evening lamb.

My work is o'er—my office hence be thine!
ABNER.
Like our false sires when Moses smote the rock,
For living streams, I had the murmuring lip.
Cleansed now my stain, but not by me forgot,
I vow that I will wed my priestly work,
And to Jehovah's glory give my life!

Enter ONO *and* EVA.

ELI.
My children, blest by Heaven, and in yourselves
I thought I heard your voices murmuring near;
Ono, thine arm proves royal as thy blood,
And fit thy brow to wear King David's crown:
Our Eva happy, shelter'd at thy side!
Happy your home, hung round by fragrant bloom!
Oh, lead me where my own long wedded years
Flew wing'd with joy, and tell me as we go
How looks in brilliant beauty forth our land,
Which on these longing eyes may smile no more!

[ONO *and* EVA *kiss and embrace* ELI, *and conduct him to their home, while* ABNER *remains in the cloister.*

How sweet the breath of this fresh evening air
That whispering lifts the locks from my old brow!

EVA.
How Olivet doth glow, tipp'd by the sun,

While gorge and cliff flash back his golden light!
ELI.
In boyhood oft I climb'd his hoary sides,
And chased from rock to rock the brown gazelle.
ONO.
And there, like one long line of waving gold,
The queen of seas lies waiting for the stars,
That soon will find a mirror in her face.
ELI.
Once those same waves I saw from Carmel's top
Where our Elijah knelt and open'd heaven.
EVA.
One fitful gleam shows where the Dead Sea sleeps.
Then settles o'er the South a hiding haze.
ELI.
Oft on those shores, still as my grave will be
And void of life, I've bent my musing steps—
While mem'ry saw the flames roll o'er in doom.
ONO.
Sweet in his silver Jordan winds along,
Bloom on his banks, and music in his song;
Soon o'er his hills will climb the clustering vine;
Soon in his vales will golden harvests shine.
Judea's life is from his murmuring flow,
Where hope now brightens in yon sunset glow.
ELI.
Oh, that these eyes could see the beauty there!

Yet memory still recalls the scenes so fair,
Where my young manhood led my brilliant bride
Bright as the roses on the river's side.

EVA.

The sun's last glance is on Siloam's pool,
That seems a glittering gem in emerald set,
While Cedron dashes on in mountain glee;
The temple-hill shines with resplendent glow,
As when Jehovah gleam'd there through His cloud.
From our new altar its first flash of fire!
Lo, o'er its smoke a rainbow smiling bends,
And down on Israel sheds the light of hope.

ELI.

I weary grow, and on some stone must rest:
Here I will sit, and tell my dream to you.
As I lay sleeping in my cloister'd nook,
I thought I saw our temple rise once more.
Low linger'd in mine ear that chanted psalm
Sung oft responsive by our white-robed choirs,
Where comes the King of Glory from his gates.
Soothed by the warbled sounds I smiled with joy.
Its altar earth, and the starr'd heaven its dome,
Jehovah's house grew to the universe.
Then One, who was our God, and yet was man,
Died 'mid a gloom that robed our shaking world;
But soon burst from his grave, and rose to Heaven,
Resplendent there, and everlasting Priest:

Anon, on clouds He came, 'mid angels throned,
In flashing might, to sit majestic Judge;
Last, earth was wrapp'd in fire, and from the blaze
A new world rose in an immortal bloom,
And saints and cherubim with songs adored
Him, ever King, both Human and Divine.

FAITH.

FAITH.

HAT curious bosom never throbb'd to roll
Mysterious darkness from the burden'd soul?
Who would not tear his being's veil away,
And burst to light in truth's eternal day?
O, who glows not with burning wish to find
Where tend these restless energies of mind—
Where point these mystic longings and desires
That hide in every breast their wasting fires?

Faith lifts each cloud, the void of life supplies,
Sheds light o'er earth, and leads on to the skies.

What secret power, with universal force,
Can atoms join, and worlds keep in their course?
True as the spell that points to Heav'n a soul
What makes the needle tremble to the pole,—
Beams in the twilight star with golden ray,

And flashing from the sun sheds round the day?
Or tell, what power invisible can bind
Insentient matter to immortal mind?
Lo, Science points where, quivering on the sky,
With vivid joy the frantic lightnings fly,
And finds through worlds electric forces reign
That bind creation in one mystic chain.
Thus in the spirit-realm with sovereign sway
Faith rules and calls its energies in play—
O'er all the unseen empire has control,
Explains, pervades, and regulates the whole.

Turn where we may, the curious eye surveys
Through the wide circles of the social maze—
From the lone hut where squalid misery pines
To where in pride the splendid palace shines,
From the drear isle where rude barbarians dwell
To lands where Science breathes her magic spell,—
Each human link in the vast living round
To the whole chain by Heaven's own wisdom
   bound,
Till trust in others from our infant breath,
Through all life's sorrows to the shades of death,
Joins man to man, forms ties of sacred love,
And points us to eternal worlds above.

Faith, too, in self, when obstacles oppose,
Which in the breast of modest genius glows,

FAITH. 203

Alone can fire the daring soul for flight
Beyond the clouds that veil the fields of light.
Let dark Distrust enjoy her shadowy reign,
Let fears of failure haunt the troubled brain,
The arm will lose its force, the mind its fire,
And every lofty scheme in night expire.
When Danger scowls, when Penury's chill frown
Palsies the heart and weighs the spirit down,
When withering scorn, the jeer of silly mirth
Would drag the bold adventurer back to earth,
O'er doubts triumphant and unmoved by sneers
His lifted eye will brighten 'mid its tears,
And high on Faith's exultant wing he'll rise
To drop in love his mantle from the skies.

Behold Columbus spread his venturous sail
Where mountain-billows sweep before the gale!
Ye light'nings, clouds, and tempests, all in vain
Ye flash and frown and roar along the main!
Let earth and sea and sky mix in the strife,
Let murder plot and grasp the secret knife,
Serene the hero's soul, erect his form,
Through the wild ragings of the midnight storm.
While gathering perils dark around him spread,
Faith sheds her awful brightness on his head;
" Onward! " he cries; God smiles upon the brave:
No tempests more can toss the sleeping wave,

And soon with raptured glance his eyes explore
The misty outlines of the promised shore.

Celestial Faith! thy guardian hand appears
And points great Newton to yon wheeling spheres;
A halo binds around his brow serene
As he surveys the glittering starry scene,
Darts his keen eye through the wide realms of space,
And takes creation in his mind's embrace.

Amid the battle-cloud, as freemen fight,
I see thy hovering form crown'd with the light.
While Briton's lion glaring crouches low,
And footprints mark with blood the shining snow;
While low-brow'd Treason hides with specious smiles
A soul which gold has bought, and plans his wiles;
While Disaffection murmurs through the land,
Chills Freedom's heart and weakens Freedom's hand;
While patriots groan, while shrieking Hope takes flight,
To leave the world in an eternal night,
From Heav'n I hear thy glad inspiring cry—
"Fight on, ye brave! your cause shall never die!"
From thy bright realms I see thee bring relief,

And seek on wings of love our matchless chief;
Smile through the storm, and bid him stand unawed,
And trust his country to his country's God.

Illustrious Hope! with brighten'd glance mine eyes
Thy glittering pinions see wave on the skies;
Soon radiant stands thy graceful image where
Yon son of genius sinks into despair;
'Tis thine, indeed, to bid the shades depart
That cloud his brow and agonize his heart:
'Tis thine with glowing pictures to inflame
Immortal ardours for the wreath of Fame:
'Tis thine the Future's curtain to unroll,
And stream its glories o'er the hero's soul;
But soon thy colours fade, thy visions fly,
Like painted vapours when a breeze may sigh,
Unless, with loftier eye and nobler mien,
Majestic Faith descends to rule the scene.

Yes! thou inspiring Faith, in trial's day,
When night draws round, and storms burst on our way;
When from their depths in rage wild oceans rise,
And dash their fury up to trembling skies;
Thou, Faith, like Him, whose majesty confess'd

Hush'd by one monarch-word the waves to rest,
Dost calm our fears, dost turn our raptured sight
Where tempests never sweep in paths of night.

Let, blissful Faith, thy magic wand but wave,
Point through the cross to Him beyond the grave,
Griefs bloom with joys, bright rainbow-lustres
    play,
Despair will smile, and midnight turn to day.

Fidelio's mansion blush'd once in the dawn,
Whose morning light glow'd crimson o'er his lawn;
Religion on his home her glory shed,
And Art and Learning round their graces spread;
Shall storms arise? shall sorrow shed her tear
O'er scenes of bliss unclouded by a fear?
Lo, slander blasts, the mob a torch applies,
Above his home flames leap to midnight skies;
Fidelio's wife glares with a maniac gaze;
Fidelio's children perish in the blaze.
About Fidelio, guiltless, clanks a chain,
And wretches taunt him with red murder's stain.
" Oh, Heaven," he cries, " with vengeance-burning
    dart,
Why dost thou love to pierce and pain my heart?"
Lo, while he speaks, see in the glimmering ray

FAITH.

That through his dungeon-bars finds dim its way,
A smile is on his face, his features shine
As round him plays a flood of light divine;
Faith looks aloft to One whose eye is there,
And glory gilds the shadows of despair.
" Father, smite on !" Fidelio's lips exclaim ;
" All shall be known when earth is wrapp'd in
    flame ;
Yes! then thy hand the curtain shall unroll,
To show why sorrow thus has wrung my soul.
When peals thy trumpet the eternal morn,
And with its breath our world to bliss is born ;
There will we meet, immortal in the sky,
Where Love can drop no tear o'er those who die."

See, as they part, a mother kiss her boy,
While sighs delay the word that clouds her joy !
She cries, while from her eyes the tears will flow,
As clasp her arms the form most dear below,
" My son, when first thy little lip I press'd
But Heav'n can know the bliss within my breast—
The joy that thrill'd, the love and mingled pride,
As stretch'd thy hands above thy cradle's side,
While o'er thy cheeks bright smiles the roses chase
That seem'd caught from thy hovering angel's face.
Laid on the grass I see thine image now,
And boyhood's curls wave clustering o'er thy brow.

Oh trust, my son, since Manhood bids us part,
And veils with sorrow's shade my widow'd heart,
When tempests darken trial's winter-day,
Thy father's God and thine will guard thy way!"
He goes, while filial tears his cheeks suffuse,
Flush'd with gay hopes his path of life to choose;
And when Temptation spreads her glittering snare,
When Pleasure smiles to drag him to despair,
Maternal Faith, his shield in peril's hour,
Defies a world, and baffles demon-power.

And when tornadoes burst from angry clouds,
When lightnings leap across the vessel's shrouds,
When thunders peal wild answers to the waves,
And ocean lash'd to madness yawns with graves,
When Hope forsakes, and agonizing cries
Above the battling elements arise,
The wife at home bids storms no longer blow;
Her Faith chains down the seas that heave below,
And spreads the sail, and makes the willing breeze
Speed him most loved safe over glittering seas.

Blest child of Faith, whose smile is o'er the
skies,
Robed in her morn Love brightens on mine eyes!
Wide to the breeze her standard be unfurl'd,
To wave its peaceful glories o'er our world!

FAITH.

What breast the brilliant vision never knew
That gilds earth's clouds with Hope's inspiring
    hue?
O say, who ne'er the future's veil unroll'd
To see return again the age of gold?
From time's first dawn the varied cycles share
The same old dream that lifts man from despair,
Since in his soul th' immortal wish has birth,
That yearns the glow of Heav'n to find on earth.

What power omnipotent shall burst our chain,
And o'er our world shall spread the splendid
    reign?
Can Science with her orient ray dispel
A gloom that blackens from the shades of
    hell?
Oh! Reason, in her wisest laws express'd,
Is vain to tame the passions of the breast,
To bind wild nations to her stately car,
Or wreathe the olive round the sword of war.
Thou, matchless Faith, thou, wing'd with thine
    own light,
Must flash away the clouds that make our night;
Thou from despair must give to man release
Till Love shall spread o'er earth the sway of
    Peace!

P

But frowning here, a phantom-form appears
To cast her shadow o'er the future years.
"Judge from the Past, deluded man," she cries:
'Hope's glittering visions but deceive thine eyes;
Poor dupe of priests, no promis'd day shall shed
Millennial brightness on thy suffering head!"

Paint, Infidelity, in darkest hues,
Paint from the past thy soul-contracting views;
Then in the cheerless colours of the tomb
Let thy despairing picture frown in gloom,
While lightning-flashes o'er its blackness dart
More fierce than hate that burns within thine
       heart!
On mountains mountains pile along the way
Where Faith points on to a thick millennial day!
Thy art is vain! no shades at thy command,
No demon-touches from thy master's hand,
E'er sketch'd such paths of blood, such seas of fire
As Heav'n arrays when prophets sweep her lyre.

But shall Faith tremble at the dread survey
And turn aghast her wilder'd eye away—
To passion's power, to Satan's sway give o'er
Immortal men, chain'd down for evermore?
Nay! from the skies majestic scenes unfold;
Faith sees her angels wave their wings of gold;

FAITH.

Then, rank on shining rank, from Heav'n descend,
And with her wrestling sons in battle blend.
Above the strife behold her towering form,
Calm as some sunlit rock amid a storm,
While in her hand th' Eternal Word appears
To gild earth's darkness with sabbatic years;
And as the scenes of future bliss arise,
Light crowns her brow and kindles in her eyes!

'Twas thus when morn dispell'd the midnight's
   tears,
And glanced in terror on the Syrian spears,
As gathering foes 'mid yells of clamorous hate
With axes thunder at the trembling gate,
The Prophet, smiling, turns aloft his gaze
Where chariots burn, celestial warriors blaze.

From Heav'n's bright hills, Faith sends her
   clarion-cry,
And angel-forms again are on the sky—
" Ye Christian soldiers, go—your standard raise
Till over earth millennial glories blaze!
Where stormy winters sweep around the pole,
And suns unsetting weary circles roll;
Where Nature painted in her torrid ray
Seems gorgeous as the cloud-gates of the day,
Lift high the Cross! Let Brahma raise his fanes;

And Gunga's stream in blood wind through the
    plains;
Let Boodh's dark millions in their temples bend
Where white-robed priests with mystic rites attend:
Let Feejee's fires gleam through the midnight air,
To show the writhing victims of despair:
Let Moslem vengeance bolts of ruin throw,
And blood-red crescents o'er Judea glow:
Let Rome's dark spectre tower amid the gloom,
Crown'd with her flames, to make for Faith a tomb;
Yet, Heaven your shield, ye Christian-warriors, go,
The earth your battle-field and hell your foe!
Lift high the Cross, and Science soon will rise
To hail the Gospel-Angel as he flies;
And Life's immortal page send from her hand
Like seed which autumn wings across the land;
Shall nations join, and flash along her wire
Salvation's news, as with celestial fire!
Lift high the Cross! Soon War's death-trump no
    more
Shall peal its battle-notes from shore to shore:
No chain shall clank, no superstitions throw
Grim, spectral shadows o'er a world of woe!
Lift high the Cross, till Truth shall scatter night,
And Love's bright morn shed universal light—
From clime to clime one wide effulgence stream,
And Heav'n and Earth commingle in her beam!

Hero of Heav'n, the Cross whose matchless
    grace
Did conquer thee, can move and mould a race!
Speak from thy skies! When tortured Ava's
    chain,
When torrid suns pour'd fire upon thy brain,
When sadly came upon the scorching gale,
With prison-curses mix'd, thine infant's wail;
When prostrate she, thine angel—*more*, thy *wife*—
From pagan bounty held her guardian life,
Oh, then, by demons mock'd, by man oppress'd,
Tell me, could Love still reign within thy breast?
When, burst thy fetters, softest breezes now
Expand thy sail and play upon thy brow,
Beneath the moon waft o'er a placid stream
From scenes that frown like phantoms of a dream,
Shall Love still bind thee to that cruel shore?
For men who sought thy blood wilt thou care
    more?
Or weeping lone amid the Hopia shade
Where all that made earth bright for thee is laid,
Still wilt thou kneel, and pray for Burmah there?
Still shall Love triumph in thy dark despair?
Lo! frowns Helena o'er the sullen wave,
And Sorrow's tear drops on another grave;
Still shall thy sobbing voice the cry repeat?
Still shall thy heart with love's pulsations beat?

Still shall thy lingering eye look o'er the sea?
Still burns the wish that Burmah shall be free?
Let gold allure, let Satan in thy way
His mountains pile on Burmah's path to-day,
In Burmah's tongue th' Eternal Word must fly:
On Burmah's soil thy sleeping dust would lie!
Oh, victor thou, on some celestial height
Where play the splendours of immortal light,
As down to earth thy longing eyes explore,
They yet shall see Love reign on Burmah's shore:
On Ava's turrets yet the Cross shall rise,
And Burmah peal her anthems to the skies!

All-conquering Faith! thy hand has tamed the
    wave,
Has snatch'd from death, and burst the awful
    grave:
Thy word has calm'd the tempest's boisterous force,
And stopp'd the sun in his eternal course;
Nay! moved the arm that guides with boundless
    might
This vast creation in its onward flight;
And thou must rule with matchless power and art
The warring passions of a human heart;
Yes! thy omnipotence alone can bind
The waves and tempests of a deathless mind!

The great Napoleon on his weary rock—
Hush'd now the victor's shout and battle-shock—
A captive now amid the sea confined,
No schemes of conquest darkening now his mind,
As meditation o'er life's evening threw
A wisdom mad ambition's noon ne'er knew,
While down through vistas in the clouds of time
Eternal rays gild o'er the scene sublime—
Napoleon saw that Force with tyrant sway,
Might briefly make reluctant man obey,
But only Love's omnipotent control
Could found enduring empire in the soul.

Offspring of Faith, bright Love, descend and
    bring
A world in tears to kneel before her King!
By his blest sceptre touch'd, thou shalt arise,
And fling thy conquering banner to the skies.

Far-glancing Faith! let Science from her throne
Unveil earth's wonders round from zone to zone;
On tireless pinions bear the spirit far
To circle space and visit every star:
Let venturous Fancy sweep on bolder wing,
Beyond where reason soars, or angels sing—
All theirs is thine—but wider thy embrace!
Yon glittering worlds shall weary in their race,

This earth shall burn, the skies shall melt away,
And o'er creation Ruin's flames shall play,
Yet from the wreck of fire thy glance descries
New systems spring, immortal glories rise!

THE ROMAN MARTYRS.

THE ROMAN MARTYRS.

TH' eternal city burns in evening light!
   See on the Pincian play its tremulous
      beams
   That gild the Capitol's majestic height,
And Coliseum flood with living streams!
Each pillar'd temple bathed in glory seems,
And whitest marbles turn to sudden gold.
Round god and hero day's last brilliance gleams
While wave on wave the dying splendours roll'd,
Rome shines like sunlit clouds, most dazzling to
      behold.

The curtains of the night fall round, how soon!
The evening star is o'er the Pantheon seen,
And Cæsar's palace silvers in the moon,
Whose radiance trembling in its yellow sheen
On garden-statues rests and groves of green;

Bright Heav'n is mirror'd now in Tiber's wave,
And tranquil grows the solemn moonlit scene;
In silent shadows mute the branches wave,
And lo, the stillness makes the city seem a grave!

Hark! laugh and jest now through the windows fly!
And merry songs peal down the quiet street,
And lute and harp unite their melody
For wall and arch their echoes to repeat.
See, waving lights in fiery circles meet,
Torch flashing after torch its wildering glare,
And curious crowds a wedding party greet,
While as they pass along 'mid shout and stare
Bright flames to Heav'n send up the joy that kindles there!

How dance upon the Bride quick-quivering rays!
Gem-clasp'd, around her form a veil of white,
With purple fringe, floats in the blaze,
And jewels, catching splendours from the light,
Like sparkling stars shine on the gloom of night;
Her snowy hands a useful distaff hold,
And smile and eye and grace inspire delight—
Cecilia's beauty not from art, nor gold;
A thought from Heav'n she moves, shaped in an earthly mould.

She looks as I have seen a queenly rose,
Blushing not yet in its maturest bloom,
When in the summer morn it waves and glows,
Or in the brilliance from some festive room,
That through the night doth tremble into gloom.
More sweet the fragrant *promise* of its leaves
Than riper glories which are near their tomb.
How nameless is the charm that fancy weaves
When simple girlhood's breast first with the
    woman heaves!

Moves by Cecilia's side Valerian's form
From which a toga's graceful folds depend;
He seems a youthful tree that braves the storm
On mountains, when the thunderbolts descend
'Mid lightning-flames, and crashing, scathe and
    rend.
The blood of Pompey fills Cecilia's veins,
Valerian's eyes fierce Julian flashes send;
Rome hears exulting their glad marriage strains,
And Hope smiles from the cloud which on the
    empire stains.

Before Valerian's home at last they stand,
Where clustering flowers hang mingling scents
    and hues.
What odorous beauty there doth Love command,

Shining like leaves bathed in their morning dews!
A world, indeed, is blushing round profuse,
And glows more brightly as the flames advance.
The bloom of each gay clime the eye may choose :
Or smiling sweetly in the moon's cold glance,
Or lifted by a breeze the torch-lit leaves do dance.

Not only, Rome, thine eagles from a world
Did bring the vase, and coin, and flashing gem ;
Not only did thy banner high unfurl'd
Wave over plunder'd throne and diadem ;
Not only did thy legions kingdoms hem,
And bear to thee their spoil from every side ;
Not only temples did thy lust condemn,
But pilfer'd flowers did e'en thy ravage chide,
Pluck'd forth from every land to deck thy festive
pride !

The Bride stops trembling at Valerian's door ;
Sweet modesty sits blushing in her face ;
The husband draws with gentle force before,
Charm'd with Cecilia's scarce-resisting grace.
In her new home the wife soon finds a place
That makes the timid girl a matron now ;
With joy friends clasp her in their warm embrace
Till shakes the flower-crown on her queenly brow,
While held in her white hands her keys her reign
avow.

Valerian and Cecilia both receive
The Faith of Him who, slain, is yet divine;
Nor when they in the crucified believe,
Do they to cold austerities incline.
Love o'er their lives his gentleness did twine :
True to the cross, the crown their joy inspires ;
Around their home bright Christian graces shine:
To others bless, theirs, toil that never tires—
That earth her King may own, they glow with
    ceaseless fires.

Thus from one root two vines spring side by side,
Lifting their graceful branches wide and high;
One strong and stately towers in loftier pride,
Round which the other, fairer, seeks the sky,
And clings more closely when the storm roars by.
From the same light and dew their scent and
    bloom ;
Through kindred veins the same life-currents
    ply,
And when Decay has fix'd their fatal doom,
They intertwining lie on earth, the same sad tomb.

Has ever Faith escaped the bursting storm ?
Not in the shelter'd vale the sturdiest tree
Rears into heav'n its tall majestic form.
Its roots love mountain-rocks, its branches see

Waving o'er clouds, where lightnings, wild and
    free,
Fling round their wrath—the elemental glee
It courts and dares, while under skies o'ercast
It grows, and spreads e'en while the tempest
    thunders past!

Where Christians would elude their murderous
    foes
Hid far beneath the fatal stare of day,
Valerian, taught by his Cecilia, goes,
To find the holy rites without delay.
His splendid toga changed for sober gray,
Down from a suburb garden he descends;
A lamp directs his solitary way,
Whose glimmering circle to the darkness lends
A glare, as he along his path in silence wends.

Grows fainter on his ear the city's sound
As ocean billows when we leave the shore,
Or mountain-torrents hurling thunders round,
In distance mellow their eternal roar.
The fading hum at last is heard no more:
There rattles down the noise of hoof and car,
And bursting through the cavern's open door
Subdued, a shout is rushing from afar
Where, laurel-crown'd, 'mid spoils, a victor show
    his scar.

That shout the Julian in Valerian woke:
His breath comes panting, and his heart throbs
    fast,
As dreams of glory o'er his vision broke
Like clouds sun-gilded when a storm has pass'd,
Whose burning splendours dazzle while they
    last.
He could have conquer'd 'neath the eagle's eye,
And rush'd to fame upon war's tempest-blast:
He could have heard *his* name borne to the
    sky,
And roll'd along through Rome the triumph proud
    and high.

For crowns now chains: for glory now this
    gloom;
Now for the altar-fire the martyr-blaze,
And for the palace now the catacomb
Where buried exiles drag out weary days:
And flames and prisons rush before his gaze
Till pain-drops burst and bathe his quivering
    form.
He stops, he gasps, he kneels, he trusts, he
    prays;
When hush'd to peace the fury of that storm,
Hope's pulses through youth's veins beat strong,
    and fast, and warm.

On through the darkness, nor despairing more,
Valerian farther winds into the night:
Above, the glare of Rome and thundering roar:
Beneath, death's empire in his lamp's pale light.
City of tombs! where martyrs for the right
From tyrants were conceal'd deep in the earth;
Or scathed by flames, or scarr'd in deadly fight,
Thy memories nobler of heroic worth
Than purpled Cæsars boast who claim imperial
    birth!

Oh, sacred dust, tier rising over tier!
With reverent step, Valerian, thou must tread!
Here sleeps a father borne on blood-stain'd bier.
And here his son stung by the asp till dead:
One sword-pierced here who on th' arena
    bled,
While near him coffin'd lies his strangled bride.
This martyr to a corpse was manacled:
And babe and mother slumber side by side
With soldiers of the faith who chain and fire
    defied.

Now distant lights glance on Valerian's gaze
Whose circles throw around a flickering gleam,
But shine, as he goes on, with larger blaze,
    And sounds grow louder in the brightening
    beam,

Which words of worship soon distinctly seem.
Hark! mingling voices yet more clear and
    strong
Their praises pour, and bursting swell and
    stream
High to the roof, then echoing far along,
Roll through that cavern's night to Heav'n the
    Christian song.

The people kneel, and their low murmur dies
As if should cease the solemn roar of seas,
Or stop the winds, which, sweeping autumn
    skies
Tell yet of stormier blasts to shake the trees.
Valerian hears, borne on devotion's breeze,
A prayer, faith-wafted far, in love's soft tone,
And knows an Eye omniscient watchful sees.
Oh, safe is he, if world on world be thrown,
Since e'en 'mid nature's wreck a Father keeps his
    own.

As parts the crowd Valerian forward goes
Clothed in baptismal robes of glittering white:
Peace in his silent heart divinely flows,
And joy beams shining o'er his trial's night;
Around his brow a coronal of light.
He kneels by sacred drops for ever seal'd

A martyr-soldier in the Christian fight—
Hope, Truth, and Faith his helm, and sword,
    and shield—
Those arms which Heaven bestows for earth's
    contested field.

Our duty done, the soul how strong and bright!
So shines a mountain in morn's gilding beam
Lifting its brilliant head calm through the light,
While 'neath it thunders peal and light'nings
    gleam,
And madden'd torrents hear the eagle's scream.
Oh! yet, as roar the clouds by tempests whirl'd,
More beautiful those glittering summits seem
That tower from gloom where vengeance round
    is hurl'd,
And crown'd with sparkling snows, stand monarchs
    of the world.

When through the city it was spread by fame
Valerian and his Bride had Christ confess'd,
Most madly burn'd the universal flame—
From slave to monarch vengeance in each
    breast;
The temple's priest and suppliant rage
    express'd—
He who adorn'd the shrine, and who adored,

And who the victims sold, or victims bless'd,
Till through each rank the blaze of malice soar'd,
And round Rome's pontiff-throne its selfish fury
    pour'd.

Thus I have seen a flame creep o'er a vale
And slowly climb along some towering height,
Wavering, and glimmering, and in sunbeams
    pale;
But fierce and reddening with the storm and
    night
It higher flashes, wider and more bright,
Until it roars, billows on billows hurl'd,
And burns that mount, a pyramid of light
Whose top is fire by tempests dash'd and whirl'd,
While wild destructions blaze to terrify a world.

Into the Coliseum now is rushing Rome;
Behold the mighty pile majestic stand,
Lifting its wall without a roof or dome
Above the pigmied crowd, silent and grand;
Type of a Power that can a world command,
Rising to heav'n a monument of gloom,
Whose shadows darken earth's remotest land;
Glowing and pack'd with life, and yet a tomb
Where nations see their sons dragg'd to a bloody
    doom.

The circling crowd, all-madden'd, sways and
   heaves,
And whisper'd murmurs swell to stormy cries,
As I have seen on tapering boughs the leaves
Quiver and tinkle when the breeze first sighs,
Which soon, a tempest turn'd, sweeps o'er the
   skies;
Branch shrieks to branch, the tossing forest
   roars,
And as the splinter'd fragment whirls and flies,
Higher and farther yet the fury pours,
Till bursting to the clouds a whirlwind's tumult
   soars.

How can a Christian into future woe
A spirit lost and lone for ever send,
When his own soul, unfetter'd by the blow,
On wing of light would up to heav'n ascend,
Soaring where saint and seraph shine and blend?
His weapons dash'd to earth, Valerian stands,
While circling angels round in love do bend,
   And placed across his breast his folded hands,
That multitude to awe his majesty commands.

See, from his face immortal lustre streams,
And on his head a diadem of light!
Around his form a dazzling glory beams

As if an angel stood before our sight,
Whom Truth had arm'd to battle for the right.
With weapons poised, three trembling wretches
    now,
Before such goodness pale, pause in their fright,
While grows the brilliance on Valerian's brow
As Heav'n, with its own crown, approves the
    martyr's vow.

The monarch's signs and people's rising rage
From tier to circling tier, soon break the spell,
And then, like wild beasts rushing from their
    cage,
The gladiators strike with blow and yell
And fury kindled by a spark of hell.
Valerian, wounded, staggers o'er the ground,
Where left in slippery blood a lion fell,
Then sinking on the beast with gasping sound
He waves a silver cross in holy triumph round.

As touch'd by evening's ray that Christian sign
Around the Coliseum gleams and glows,
With brilliance glittering which appear'd divine,
And o'er the crowd defiant splendour throws;
From rank to rank wild flames of hate arose
Till never Ætna blazed when earthquakes rend
Its sides of rock, and down red lava flows,

And flashing to the clouds its fires ascend,
Like those indignant tiers where hate and rage do blend.

Swift through the storm Valerian's spirit goes
By angels guided into blissful skies,
And looking downward, smiling, sees its foes,
And higher mounting faintly hears their cries,
While they behold his clay with furious eyes.
A monarch's frown, an empire's rage how small
To him, who soaring through earth's clouds, descries
The glittering battlements of heav'n's bright wall,
And that Eternal King who is the light of all!

And while Valerian thus has met his doom,
Cecilia sits and views the golden west,
And reads her death in its fast-gathering gloom.
In white baptismal robes behold her dress'd!
A golden crucifix is on her breast,
And on her hair a virgin fillet bound
Whose clasp a wedding diamond shines confess'd.
Day's lingering lustre o'er her head streams round,
And floating to her room sweet strains angelic sound.

Chamber and Coliseum share the rage
Against the Cross, waked by imperial power,
Which, all-relentless, spares nor sex nor age,
As storms hurl Alpine trees which high may tower
To greet the sun, and crush the nestling flower
That looks aloft with its blue trembling eye,
Till madly when the roaring heav'ns do lower,
The bright and scented leaves will whirl and fly
With limbs of giant pines dash'd o'er the blacken'd sky.

If torn that flower, if spoil'd its fragrant bloom
When darkens over earth the storm's wild wing,
It is not swept to an eternal tomb;
But fierce tornadoes will its seeds far fling
O'er a wide world, and thus gay beauties bring
To brighten empires through each distant age;
And budding out of death truth thus will spring
When error's battles sceptred monarchs wage,
And scatter life-germs round e'en on the tempest's rage.

Lictor and Lady face to face do stand
Alone within her chamber's hallow'd space.
A glittering sword grasp'd in his lifted hand,
He strong in arm, and terrible in face;

Cecilia frail, in woman's softest grace;
He a low wretch cloth'd with an empire's might;
She doom'd, and yet of Pompey's splendid race;
He stands a man, now pale with tremulous fright,
While she an angel smiles in innocence and light.

Thrice strikes the Lictor that pure breast of snow
Heaving beneath its white baptismal fold,
When, gushing out, the crimson currents flow,
And to the floor in martyr-drops are roll'd,
Staining the path of faith to joy untold.
Cecilia falls, and glory round her gleams;
Hark! seraph-music breathes from harps of gold,
And on her face celestial radiance streams
Which Christ has flash'd o'er death in bright, immortal beams.

Sailing upon the blue of evening's sky
Oft I have seen a cloud of spotless white,
Which stopp'd, with yet no brilliance for the eye,
But as the sun, his face enlarged and bright,
Pour'd forth in levell'd floods his parting light
. Into those mists, they take his blaze, and burn

Till Heav'n seems shining down on mortal
    sight:
And thus o'er dying saints some halo plays
From that Diviner Orb whence stream eternal rays.

Cecilia's spirit softly breathes away
By seraphs wafted on low warbled strains,
To float in melodies where endless day
Its glory flashes o'er celestial plains,
And never yet have come Time's cares or pains.
She dies like sound on some Æolian string,
Whose lingering whisper in the ear remains,
Fading from earth in faintest murmuring
As if in heaven to burst, and thrill where angels
    sing.

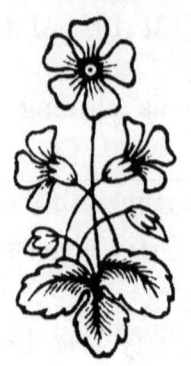

THE DELUGE.

THE DELUGE.

ON wood where burst a storm when
    Adam pass'd
Accurs'd through Eden's gate, now
    echoes back
The axe's constant stroke, and gophers shake
Their towering tops, then thunder to the ground.
See patient oxen draw the weary load,
And pile the plain around that man whose brow
Has felt the tempests of six hundred years!
Since first the mountain heard his sturdy blows
Twelve crescent moons have silver'd o'er the sky,
Then turn'd their fuller circles into gold.
Crowds view the work. Doth here a palace rise,
Or hence shall glittering tower a temple's dome?
Silent the patriarch toils, until his hand
Has shaped a mighty Ark, heav'd high in air,
And made to breast the storm and ride the wave.

What shouts of scornful laughter shake the
   skies!
Now from beyond the flood I hear their taunts—
"Ha, venerable fool, what turns thy brain?
Where spreads a sea to float th' unwieldy hulk?
Or wilt thou sail her on these burning sands?
Or shall the sky drop oceans from above,
Or wilt thou call them from earth's bursting
   breast?"
'Tis winter in thy heart, remorseless Scorn!
Thy smile disdainful chills the tides of life,
And merit withers at thy icy touch;
Yea! thou hast snatch'd away the martyr's crown,
And laugh'd to shut on him the gate of Life.

   I see the patriarch kneel, and while his tears
Drop on the floor, his modest prayer ascends,
And soon are hush'd the tempests of his breast.
Joy lights his soul, and vigour nerves his arm,
Till on the beam loud rings his hammer's stroke:
And when the crowd may mock, he mounts his ark
To blend love's warning with a prophet's awe.

   On him whom Heav'n gives o'er 'tis sad to gaze.
Bright health may pencil beauty on his cheek,
And grace breathe o'er his acts, and he may shine
A star whose glory wide the nations praise:

Yet draw the veil! He walks amid a cloud;
And drags a coffin to each scene of joy.
A mother's tear can bring no answering drop;
A father's prayer falls back on silenced lips;
And night's eternal shadow settles round.

If like a tree stripp'd of its brilliant bloom,
And black with blasting fire and struck by death,
Tossing its moaning branches in the gloom,
One thus foredoom'd, what then a teeming world!
Death laughs to hear its song, and lures it on
To darker woe, and grins where hearthstones blaze.
As maidens crown the bride, he blasts the flowers,
And from his cloud, while thunders scare, he cries,
"Hail, my gay children, hail! Wave high the
   torch,
Swim through the dance, and drink the purple wine:
Make bright a world which soon will prove a
   tomb;
Wear garlands gay, and deck your paths to me!"

In such a world long did the patriarch toil;
None heard beyond his home, and on the stream,
Wild, turbulent, and dark, roll'd over earth.
Yet leans he on the hand that made the sun;
Faith hears from future years a voice of joy,
And sees an altar by a rainbow spann'd.

Behold his work achieved! As some lone isle
Heaved up by earthquakes from a tropic deep,
Lifts high its rocks, and scorns the battling sea,
Thus that majestic Ark towers o'er the plain,
And dares from sky and earth their torrent floods.

Trees which had stood while yet the sun was
  young,
And Adam shelter'd with their monarch-boughs,
That vessel form. Three stories make three halls ;
Through one large window comes the light of
  heav'n—
No need of more when all the sky is cloud—
No sun, nor moon, nor star to pierce the gloom,
Whose shadows soon will mantle round a world.
Maybe, bright pendent lamps dispell'd the night:
Maybe, Jehovah's presence was the day.
One door was there for all life spared on earth.
From fires, pitch roll'd its smoke, and on each
  seam
In ladles pour'd, made black the lofty Ark,
Bidding defiance to the coming floods;
Piled high within the wealth of summers lies
To save our world from universal death.

See near the Ark that pair whence came our
  race!

'Mid sadness and despair I hear a cry:
"Ah! why this toil? Why thus wear out thy
 strength?
Why store this Ark, and starve thy wife and sons?
They grudge each stroke, amid the scorn of foes;
Cease thy vain work—thy silly Ark tear down,
And use its harvests for thyself, and us!
Or let yon altar-brand light up its flames,
That it no more may kindle for us hate!
Most vain thy dreams! Nor bird, nor beast will
 come,
Self-moved, from distant lands to seek thy Ark."

A beam of glory gilds o'er Noah's brow;
His tone is soft, yet as the trumpet clear:
"Shall God be mock'd, by whom I dare the
 world?
My work complete, shall I fling off my crown
Just when its glittering rim comes near my brow?
Should I take out my stores, or burn my Ark,
What shouts of scorn from earth would burst o'er
 me!
Jehovah I will trust while shines his sun!"

Lo! sudden thunders burst out from a wood,
And roar on roar shakes startled earth and air,
As two majestic lions stalk in view!

When morning's sun first beam'd down on their
    lair,
They started from their dens, and wander'd round,
Until, like magnet-isles which vessels draw,
Th' unconscious Ark attracts the kingly beasts.
With stately pride the long-maned monster treads,
His crouching mate submissive at his side.

New wonders rise. Two giant elephants
With twisting trunks, and tusks of gleaming
    white,
Lift swift on clumsy feet their monstrous bulk;
Between their pendent ears no riders sit.
Where Gunga rolls his wave, and banyans make
With rooted boughs their dark and pillar'd shade,
Thence were they moved, till towers the Ark in
    view.
A tiger-pair behind their stripes display,
And graceful leopards show their spotted sides.
The noble steed that paw'd Arabia's plains,
And in wide nostrils snuff'd the flying sands;
Unwieldy behemoth, the frail gazelle,
Boas that wind with speed their ponderous length,
All kinds that walk or creep from pole to pole,
And round the burning circles of the globe—
Parents of those who roam our second world—
One vast procession, troop towards the Ark.

THE DELUGE.

Low down upon the sky, behold two specks,
That soon with wings appear! As full-sail'd ships
That bound before the breeze, those condors cleave
Aloft the airy deep, then pause, and gaze,
And drop in slow gyrations on the deck.
Where now the Andes part the clouds of heav'n,
They spread their pinions on a mountain-cliff,
And left their homes to steer sublime their way.
The monarch-eagle not in circles now
Towers to the sun, but flies in even course,
Till on the pitchy roof he rests his feet;
The ostrich starting from Sahara's sands,
Lifts up his form, and plies his uncouth wings,
Borne on his lengthy limbs from dreaded death,
While peacocks drag along their rainbow plumes.
Birds gay as tropic flowers, or white as snows,
Of every size, and form, and wing, and hue,
Fast-flocking fly from all the climes of earth,
Till day is darken'd with their sounding wings,
And, cloud on cloud, down settle on the Ark.

Huge ocean-monsters gambolling on the wave,
With those in coral depths, and fish that swim
Majestic streams, or glittering glide in brooks,
Safe in their watery homes dread not the flood,
Nor feel the strange attraction lure them on.

The Ark is fill'd, and Noah cries: " Ascend
My wife and sons ! This hour repays our toil !
Jehovah praise, whose word is thus proved sure !
His love will guide o'er oceans wild with death !
Then, blow ye storms, and burst, ye torrent-floods !
Flash forth, ye lightnings! loud, ye thunders, roar !
Oh earth, farewell ! Ye hills kiss'd by the sun ;
Ye flowering vales, and sheltering trees, farewell !
Farewell, ye men o'er whom I still weep tears,
And each small thing I loved on earth, farewell !
Oh world, where Eden smiled, farewell ! farewell ! "

Hand now in hand the Prophet and his spouse,
With solemn tread and slow, ascend the Ark ;
Shem, Ham, and Japheth follow with their wives.
Jehovah shuts them in, and bars the door,
Lest they, with pity weak may draw the bolt
And rebels save whom Justice doom'd to death.

Awe like a midnight settles o'er the world ;
Pale faces dart amid the gloom, and lips
Low murmur fear. The mother grasps her child,
Press'd with convulsive shudders to her breast,
And looks with frantic gaze into the sky.
Now shrieks of men and cries of beasts burst out.
One dog's long howl rose hideous on the wind—
Yell after yell—'till silenced by a blow.
Groups view the clouds, or start when tempests
    sweep,

While conscience wakes, and Noah's warnings burst
Like thunders from the past, and earth grows still,
As if to hear her final note of doom.

The Heavens are changed. Clouds piled on
    clouds rush on,
Sweeping in mountain-masses o'er the sky,
Then mingling stand one roof of angry black.
Storm shrieks to storm—to thunders, thunders
    peal,
And lightnings blaze, and skies dash torrents down,
By column'd waters met that spout from earth,
Till murmuring brooks sweep on resistless floods,
The valleys fill, and rush along the hills;
Earth groans convulsed with pangs, and rivers bear
The houses down, and flocks and struggling men.
Wild ocean clamours now to rule the world,
And shrill despair is heard above the storms.
Crowds seek the Ark, with glaring eyeballs kneel,
And stretching out vain hands, for mercy shriek;
Some scale the pitchy sides, but baffled soon,
Down from the fatal smoothness drop to die.
Some ladders lean which envious waves wash o'er.
Others with ponderous axes cut the wood,
Till strangling waters stop their useless blows;
Some climb the trees, the roofs and towers ascend,
In frenzy vain rush screaming up the hills.

Mad floods pursue. The sudden-roaring blast,
A billow seizing by its crested top,
Soon dashes down a mountain on their heads.
Trees, hills are hid. The tall-tower'd city sinks,
And monsters swim above its ghastly dead;
One wretch, the last of earth, a summit scales
Which looks o'er all the sea, and on its top
A moment stands, seen in the lightning's glare,
With streaming hair, and tight-clench'd fists, and
    brow
That dares the storm, till billows hurl him off,
Extorting yells that louder shriek than floods:
Then Heav'n is all a cloud, and Earth a sea!

The Ark floats towering o'er the fatal waves,
And rides above the solitary world;
Amid the roar of storms hear Noah's voice:
" Jehovah praise, whose mercy gave my Ark!
Ye floods and tempests join to sound him thanks!
Ye beasts rejoice, and ye bright tuneful birds,
Who in the tree-tops sang, or in the clouds,
As once when glowing morning woke your lays
Fill with your sweetest notes my friendly Ark!
Praise Him behind your clouds, Sun, Moon and
    Stars!
Glad Angels, strike your harps and cheer our
    gloom!

Behold my Ark, pledge of the Promised Seed,
And thrill the Heav'n and Earth with joyful
 praise!"

While Cherubim admire from hills of life,
From shades of death the Prince of Night surveys.
With lip of hate, and eye that roll'd in pain
Yet gleam'd revenge, his words of scorn shook hell:
" Princes, when burst our chain, and dropp'd our
 yoke,
We malice chose for love and ill for good;
Praises to curses turn'd, and bliss to pain.
Where God would bless we blast, and where He
 saves
We counterwork to damn, and build up hell;
His Son I would hurl down and take His throne;
Nor have I fail'd against Omnipotence;
I with an apple blasted Eden's bloom,
And let in death to riot o'er a world;
By waters chill'd have millions sought my fire.
The greater task achieved, the less is sure.
But eight of earth survive—within an Ark—
Toss'd on mad waves—a plank 'twixt them and
 death!
Fly ye, and pierce that hulk! Shake Noah's faith!
Scale the black cloud and hurl the lightning-bolt!
Dash oceans down, and let wild waters in!

Let whirlwinds sweep the wreck beneath the sea!
Earth then is mine, when ends the woman's seed!
Oh, yet, unbruis'd, refulgent to the stars
My head shall tower, and wear Jehovah's crown!"

Forthwith their rushing pinions darken hell,
And they shriek round the Ark. On nimble feet
With aiding wings some climb and mount the wave
To dash it on the deck, while lightnings blaze,
And demons yell, and thunders drown the storm.
Destruction laughs, and Death rides o'er our world.

Thus Noah's faith allays each rising fear:
" When sin first blasted earth, Jehovah said,
' The woman's seed shall bruise the serpent's head.'
If sinks my groaning Ark, that promise fails,
And Hell defeats her Lord, which cannot be.
No plank shall start! no seam shall drink the
    flood!
The Hand that made the earth clasps round my Ark,
That from my loins may spring the Hope of man!
I dare thee, Hell! My God will guard His own!"

Jehovah pleased beholds His servant's faith.
Bow'd now in heav'n each knee and hush'd each
    song,

A Voice Omnipotent the silence breaks :
" My angels, see on earth that gloom of clouds
Where madden'd fiends hurl round wild waves and
    storms,
And Death rides on the blast o'er Noah's Ark !
My servant's faith has stood the shock of Hell !
Then drive those devils back, and calm the sea !
My Word shall stand ! You Ark shall save the
    world ! "

Swift down from Heav'n they drop like falling
    stars ;
And, pierced the dreadful gloom that roofs the
    world,
They light upon the waves, and range for war.
Clothed with a morning cloud, amid the gloom
Their Leader stood, bright as a sun his helm
That turn'd to stars the drops upon his wings.
His right hand grasp'd a sword, his left a trump
Of glittering gold whose blast oft peal'd o'er
    heav'n ;
Press'd to his lips, its music thrills the earth,
And makes the tempests still ; waves bow their
    heads,
The clouds take wing, the thunders sink away,
And skies are bright, and the wide ocean calm.
Scared back to hell no devil battle dares ;

With shouts of joy those angels spring through air,
Outstrip the light, and reach Jehovah's throne.

Soon dried the sea, the Ark rests on the earth
A silent witness of Eternal Love.

An angel draws the bolt, and with glad eyes
The grateful group look forth to view the world.
Hear Noah's voice: "Oh, God, my work is done!
First be to Thee my thanks, then Earth I hail!
Welcome, ye naked hills, and flowerless vales,
And mountains bleak, and bare and ragged trees!
Ye streams and oceans, let me hail you all!
Welcome, thou sun, bright morn, and gentle eve!
Spring swift, ye flowers! Ye roses, lift your heads!
Ye lilies, scent, and, daisies, deck the fields!
Come forth, thou silent grass, and robe the world!
Ye leaves, appear! Ye glowing blossoms, burst
And flush your beauty o'er the naked lands!
Oh! quick, ye harvests, wave and fruits depend,
And every varied plant adorn the scene!
Beasts, seek your fields, and, birds, cheer earth with
   song!
And go ye forth, my sons, to fill the world!
Plough the rich soil, and busy cities build;
In social commerce join sea-sever'd shores,
And make this dreary waste bloom o'er with joy!'"

THE DELUGE.

Hand now in hand come forth the aged pair—
The children next, who kneel around their sire
And kiss the earth, and fill the air with praise.
The beasts pass out and darken o'er the plain,
And birds on rushing wings fly over heav'n,
Until that Ark stands silent as a hill.

See Noah and his sons, who gather stones
Roll'd by the floods, and a square altar build!
The wood is cleft, the sacrifice is slain,
And fragrant clouds their odours waft to God,
Whose voice the stillness breaks of that young
      world:
" No more for sin shall earth be cursed by floods;
Seed-time and harvest hence, with cold and heat,
And day and night remain secure for man."

While all around the blazing altar kneel,
A sudden radiance trembling from the vale,
Rests on the mountain's brow, and climbs the
      skies,
Then bending down in vast majestic curve
With quivering glories paints the ocean's wave—
Eternal token of Jehovah's Love.

THE PERIODS.

THE PERIODS.

Canto I.

THE DAY.

MORNING.

THE twilight dim
Lines ocean's brim:
And stars from sight,
Hide in the light
Whose burnish'd gold
O'er Heav'n is roll'd.
As the sun above the sky
Lifts his royal head on high,
His beamy way
Where splendours play,
With flaming ray
Begins the day.
While the painted vapours fly
Like wild phantoms o'er the eye,

And the dew-drops glow
On the flowers bent low,
And the sunbeams flash
Where the rivers dash,
Hark! the groves warble loud
To the lark in his cloud,
As rosy MORNING's voice
Bids waking earth rejoice!

NOON.

That monarch-sun,
His course half done,
Sits throned in light
On the heav'n's height.
A crown of beams about his head;
Bright robes of glory round him spread!
Now the shadows grow small
From the quivering wall,
And field and hill
With heat are still.
How the pulse of the world beats exhausted and low!
How the breath of the world comes hard, panting, and slow!
How the face of the world is one broad, burning glow,

While the day in his ire,
Like a furnace of fire,
  Scorches Noon.

EVENING.

On the earth a holy hush,
O'er the sky a purple blush,
  Soft Eve proclaim.
Down the golden gates of day
Sinks the sun with slanted ray.
    From yon wooded hill,
    In the twilight still,
    Cries the whip-poor-will;
  The night-owl, in his oak,
  Hears the frog's solemn croak;
The crickets chirp, the beetles drum,
And earth is lull'd with insect hum.
  As shadows deeper grow,
  And the winds whisper low:
  Hush! with that fading light
  Eve sinks away in night.

·

MIDNIGHT.

The silent stars are in the sky,
The moon amid her clouds rides high,
Whose quivering light, soft, bright, and still,
Silvers the vale and bathes the hill.

Comes through the dark
The night-dog's bark,
While mortals sleep
In slumbers deep.
The fox steals forth with stealthy tread;
Beneath his wing the fowl's dull head.
Where rivers flow
The mists creep low;
Now dreams invade
From realms of shade,
As midnight's awful shadow has its birth
To wrap like death in deeper sleep the earth.

Canto II.

THE YEAR.

SPRING.

THE glowing sun now warms the breeze,
And darts his virtues through the trees
To make life-currents rise,
Which, working in the dark,
Expand the swelling bark
'Neath ever-milder skies.
Heralds of the new-born year,
See the infant buds appear!

Waked from the dead
The young leaves spread,
Till the forests of the world
Stand with banners green unfurl'd.
Broke nature's sleep,
The grasses creep,
Slow, bright, and still,
From vale to hill,
Till green robes earth with its soft dye,
As tints sweet blue the circling sky—
Hues mix'd by God to please man's eye.
Soon born the birds of every wing,
Which hop, or fly, or coo, or sing!
The streams unbound
A voice have found,
And shout around
With joyous sound,
We are free
In our glee.
Hark! blust'ring March subdued is whispering low;
Then show'ring clouds float tinged with April's
glow;
And sinking rivers glide with murmuring flow.
Flush'd with a purple ray,
Crown'd by the smiling May.
Where morning clouds in golden masses lie,
Like angels at the portals of the sky,

Beneath a rainbow's arch of splendid dye
Whose painted glories quiver in the eye—
   Brightest blossoms thy zone,
   Sweetest rose-buds thy throne,
     In a car of flowers
     Just wet with the showers,
  Ride on, thou blushing SPRING!

SUMMER.

Sprinkled with dews and showers, and warm'd
    by noon
To glory bursts the rose of fragrant June!
On the trees the leaves still denser grow,
And their silent shadows darker throw
In the longer day's intenser glow,
   While a wide-quivering haze,
   Ascending in the blaze
   As brighter burn the rays,
   Floats dream-like o'er the gaze.
Not wildly brawl the brooks, swift, wide, and deep,
But painfully slow, faint-murmuring creep;
Majestic rivers, shrunken in the sun,
Leave glaring rocks where waters cool have run.
   With dozing eye and panting side
   The ox stands meekly in the tide;
   Faint, with necks along the ground,
   Where noon-shadows lie around,

The quick-breathing sheep are found.
Low as some distance-muffled drum
The drooping city's wearied hum;
Fierce heat has hush'd the field's gay choirs,
And shrinking from day's scorching fires
Far in the wood the bird retires
Where scarce a glancing wing aspires.
 Deep the beast in his den
 Pants till night comes again;
 Without, the mountain bare
 Glows in the burning air.
 Nor now the cheery song
 As the reaper stalks along;
 Nor now shakes down the dew
 As cuts the sickle through:
 Nor now, as in the morn,
 Winds loud the harvest horn;
But like a furnace flames the sky,
And looks the sun with fiercer eye,
And lurid clouds float glaring by.
Where late o'er standing grain the sportive breezes
 play'd,
Now resting reapers dozing in the lazy shade
Amid the bearded sheaves of wheatcocks freshly
 made,
And all the yellow wealth of harvests prostrate laid
 Show brilliant SUMMER's reign.

AUTUMN.

High-piled the gather'd sheaves!
A yellow tinge in leaves!
Steals o'er the peach its flush
Deep as the evening's blush!
And when the leaves unfold
Red apples gleam o'er gold,
While on the tangled vine
The smooth, round melons shine.
Then peeping into view when lifting breezes blow,
Broad, mantling clusters on the trellis'd vineyards
    glow,
Whose streaming currents soon shall gush in
    purple flow.
    Up, with his face of blood,
    Slow o'er the deep-dyed flood,
    The sun, despoil'd of rays,
    Mounts, glaring through the haze;
    Then round with flaming glow
    Burns o'er the world below,
    Till in his evening bed
    He dips his globe of red.
Gone from the hazy air the perish'd insect's hum,
Dim phantom-pheasants in the thickets lurking
    come,
And beat the mossy log with whirring thunder-
    drum.

THE PERIODS.

      Hark! from his rail
      On morning's gale,
      The whistling quail!
With leg and tail uprear'd 'mid leaves crisp'd
    brown,
The squirrel gay his tinkling nut drops down;
And chattering swallows circling on the wing,
Debate long exile till the smile of spring,
While high the clanging wild geese floating fly,
In long-wedged squadrons through the parted sky.
    Now here and there amid the green
    A changed September leaf is seen,
    Which in eddying circles wheels
    When keen October's breath it feels,
    Or, clinging yet to its frail stem
    Until it flashes like a gem,
    Displays in morning's fresh'ning dew,
    Its yellow tinge and scarlet hue;
    And then, before November storms
    And blasting frost the world deforms,
Fields, orchards, forests, lawns, hills, plains, and
    mountains bold,
Their mingling glories to the redden'd sun unfold,
Like crimson billows flaming o'er a sea of gold,
Or Heav'n's effulgent scenes to mortal gaze
    unroll'd,
    And gorgeous AUTUMN paint.

WINTER.

Hark! shrill the blast
Fierce-sweeping past!
As wild it blows,
The shutter close!
Quick! stir the fire
Till flames aspire;
The lamp then light,
Which, shining bright,
Dark on the wall
Makes shadows fall!
The soften'd brilliance of the room
Gilds age's brow and childhood's bloom;
And curling ringlets you behold,
Hide infant smiles with waving gold.
   Without, the tempest howls;
   Without, the black sky scowls;
   Without, the beggar's form
   Is shivering in the storm,
   And from the winter-sea
   Shrieks out wild agony.
The furious winds subdued, huge leaden masses lie
Like giant spectres dimly on the silenced sky;
Then dusky clouds, weigh'd down, the noiseless
      scene bend o'er,
And the still heav'n and earth seem nearer than
      before.

THE PERIODS.

Now dropping through the air
A flake melts on your hair;
Lo! millions, soft and light,
Float on the wavering sight;
The feathery whiteness still
Descends on vale and hill;
Exhausted grows the cloud,
And earth lies in her shroud;
Fields, forests, valleys, mountains, towns, together
    show
One vast, interminable spectacle of snow.
Down the steep hill-side
See the brave boy glide!
While glad voices sing,
Sleigh-bells merry ring!
Circling o'er the sky
Let the snow-balls fly!
For the children's sport
Rise the wall and fort,
Till a warmer sun
Melts the scene of fun.
As the longer nights grow cold
Tapering icicles behold,
With their silver and their gold!
At opening day,
Where sunbeams play,
The icy trees

Flash in the breeze—
On leaf and stem
The quivering gem !
Now the stars shine small and bright
In the stillness of the night;
Now each captive stream around
Stands firm in ice-chains bound,
   And skaters glance and fly
   Beneath the moonlit sky,
And frost and snow and ice on vale and hill and plain
Show WINTER has begun his cold, remorseless reign.

Canto III.
LIFE.[1]

INFANCY.

DEEP in a cavern of the earth
   My little stream has mystic birth;
     Then flows to sight
     In morning light
Where leaning trees with arching tops ascend.
And o'er a mossy rock dim shadows blend
     With perfume
     In their gloom.

[1] Suggested by Cole's " Voyage of Life."

On waters bright to float
Emerging comes my boat;
Beneath a smiling sky
'Mid roses soft I lie,
While wings of Hours waft by.
Gay flowers on either side the waters kiss,
Whose quiet shadows sleep, the types of bliss :
Nor gentle clouds that sail above I miss,
Too fair in beauty for a world like this.
With form most bright,
And brow of light
To calm my fears,
An angel steers.
As with dimpled cheeks I glide
Where soft-rippling flows the tide,
And sweet-scented breezes chide,
Lo! heav'n's seraph-bands preside,
Waving their golden wings while childhood pure
and bright,
A brilliant morning vision, floats across the sight.

YOUTH.

Brighter the roses flush,
Deeper the clouds red blush,
As I glide
O'er the tide!

Let the angel on the land
In his foolish sorrow stand,
Since I need no more his hand!
   Adieu, every fear!
   My own boat I steer.
   Faster! ye Hours!
   Strain all your powers!
     Hands try!
     Feet ply!
     Wings vie
Till we fly, till we fly
Like clouds upon the sky!
   At my boat of oak
   Let age snarl and croak!
   Against the shore
   Let waters roar!
   With wild turmoil
   Let whirlpools boil,
   And demons stare
   In hellish glare!
See, smiling far above
Are Fame and Wealth and Love!
   Scorning measure,
   Brilliant Pleasure,
Her temple in the sky
With its dome bright and high,
A glory in the eye,
   Builds for YOUTH!

MANHOOD.

A wildering glare
  Blinds in the air!
See! bright the lightnings flash!
Hark! wild the thunders crash!
How the billows break and dash!
And the Earth wears a shroud,
And the Heaven seems a cloud;
  No angel guide
  Smiles at my side.
But, avaunt, grim Despair!
Each peril I can dare,
And my life-burden bear.
Let torrents roar and rave,
The manly and the brave
Will ride upon the wave!
Ye lightnings, swifter fly!
Storms, fiercer rend the sky!
Rush, waters, wilder by!
Your fury I defy!
  If Ruin's shock
  Creation rock,
While helps its own right hand,
In God will MANHOOD stand!

AGE.

Life's fires have ceased to glow,
My feeble pulse beats slow,
This silver'd head bows low.
    My shatter'd boat
    Just keeps afloat.
But oh! Life's Angel sheds on me his ray,
And steers my Age to his immortal day.
    While dark round me
    Rolls thy far sea,
    Eternity,
Yet, down from yon bright sky,
Through darkness thick and high,
Heav'n pours a blaze of beams
Till earth a glory seems.
A Form Divine I see round which the angels bend,
Who oft to me on waving wings in light descend.
    And soon I'll soar with them above,
Where Age shall turn immortal youth
As it beholds Incarnate Truth,
    And Life be everlasting Love.

VARIOUS PIECES.

T

VARIOUS PIECES.

OUR FLAG.

FLAG of Beauty! wide and high,
Earth saw thee given to the sky
    In Freedom's night:
Flashing then o'er battle-fires,
Thee a gazing world admires,
Onward borne by our brave sires
    To Freedom's light.

Flag of Freedom! where a spot
Darkening did thy beauty blot
    No stain we see;
Glad to Heav'n our song we raise.
Nations, swell the voice of praise!
Every star floats in the blaze
    Of Liberty.

Flag of Promise! let a world
Wide thy glories view unfurl'd,
    O'er land and sea!

Float! for ever gone thy stains!
Float! till earth has burst her chains!
Float! while Heaven bends o'er our plains
  With eagles free!

Flag of Glory! fly no more
Where 'mid death's wild thunder-roar
  Fierce brothers slay!
Glow now love where once glared ire!
Never may a star expire
Till the Heav'ns in final fire
  Have pass'd away!

OLD ENGLAND.

OLD England! Old England! our hearts
  are with thee,
 Where bright gleam thy cliffs that
  smile o'er the sea:
Old England! old England! thy blood pulses here,
And soon mingle drops by kindred made near.

Old England! Old England! thy speech is our
  own,
And sways with a power more strong than a
  throne;

Old England! Old England! thy worthies we
 know,
Who kindle our breasts with immortal glow.

Old England! Old England! a crown's on thy
 brow,
But no slave of thine a fetter feels now:
Old England! Old England! with sceptre o'er
 earth,
We hail thee the land where freedom had birth.

Old England! Old England! our faith is from
 thee,
We'll guard with our blood like those o'er the sea:
Old England! Old England! thy light in our west
Shall flash round the world like beams of the blest!

SHADOWS.

DEEP in our gleaming river,
    Amid the mirror'd trees,
  Yon elm's great branches quiver
    When rippling breathes a breeze.

Trunk, branch, and leaf appearing,
    I see inverted lie,
And shape that elm uprearing
    Its top into the sky.

Its image true is shimmering
  In its deep liquid glass;
Or dim, or bright, or glimmering
  As cloud and sunshine pass.

Thus in my soul reflected
  Far forms of Heav'n appear;
Confused, reversed, affected
  By every smile and tear.

But an eternal morning
  For these dim shapes of time,
Will show—change ever-scorning—
  Originals sublime.

THE PHOTOGRAPH.

AS you toss on your bed what strange images roll
  And chase, each the other, so grotesque, o'er the soul!
Oh! my fancies were queer, from my home far away,
And half robbing the night to make plans for the day,

Since I could not get rid of the thought for my life.
How convenient a thing is a Photograph Wife!
See the eye and the face, and the form and attire,
With those touches of taste man was made to admire;
Muff, hat, glove, and kerchief, all arranged for the fun,
And as anxious as madam to smile to the sun!
But no poutings, nor scoldings, nor feminine frown,
Like a moon in a cloud when the sun has gone down.
Take her gently—kiss the lip—look into the face
As more sweetly she smiles than a rose in a vase!
Or would wife take her leave? must we send her away?
Then no trunks are to pack and no fare-bills to pay.
Just three cents will convey her from Texas to Maine;
Just three cents bring her back, if she wishes, again;
All done in a minute—like the flash of a rocket—
Wife leaps from the mail-box and sleeps in your pocket.
Also, Photograph Children—they'll answer well too—
No combing, nor dressing, nor expense for a shoe;

No romping and bawling, and fighting and
    mussing;
No turning and twisting, and fixing and fussing;
Nor a thought for the future, nor a tear for the
    past,
Sweet and gentle and good, and besides, it will last:
Not like some young storm of Spring that sleeps
    in the sky,
But soon bursts into showers with a bang and a cry.
Indeed, such were my thoughts—I ask pardon of
    all—
These queer pranks of the mind will not stop at
    our call.
Look again at the Picture! no *soul* brightens there,
'Tis only a shadow unsubstantial as air;
A few fading lines which the sun in his play
On the paper has kiss'd with a frolicsome ray;
And that warmth of the lip and that fire of the
    eye,
And that flash of the soul like a gleam of the sky,
That soft tone of kindness when love breathes in
    the face,
And those wifely attentions bestow'd with such
    grace;
The low tender whispers far away from the crowd,
When Eve peeps with her star through the rift of
    the cloud;

And the romp and the chess and the dolls and the
    fun,
And the shout and the skates and the sleds and
    the run,
With all that is bright and sweet and lovely in
    home,
By our mem'ry made heav'n when far exiles we
    roam—
Oh yes, give me all—all—trouble, children and
    wife;
Take the smile from my lip, take the blood from
    my life,
But oh, leave those I love in Thy goodness, my God,
Who, if smitten by Thee, will yet bow to Thy rod!
Yes! when Death strikes one down, and we follow
    the bier,
As we drop on the grave the soft light of a tear,
We will look in the hope of a home to the skies,
Where the eye never weeps and the heart never
    sighs.

LIBERTY.

'TIS not the chain that makes the slave,
    Since, dared the tyrant's might,
'Mid dungeon-gloom will lie the brave
    In liberty and light.

Let Neros to their minions say—
"Go! beat, and burn, and kill!"
Their tortures, which the flesh may slay,
Give vigour to the will.

Oh! crown'd by truth, the man behold
Majestic in his chain;
Unawed by power, unbought by gold,
Unterrified by pain!

If wrong a universe could pile
On his pure honest soul,
Immortal, he would trust and smile
Uncrush'd beneath the whole.

OUR COUNTRY.

COME, Freedom's sons! unite
Beneath our Flag of Light,
One, strong, and true!
Ours is the furnace-blast;
Ours is the old world's past;
Ours is the work to cast
All into new!

Ye men of every race,
Where wave our stars find place
  And hope and rest!
Your blood with ours must flow;
Your life with ours must grow
Till we a manhood show,
  Earth's last and best.

'Twas o'er the far East first
The light of Empire burst
  With orient gleams:
But *Westward* since its way!
Let here its glories stay,
Back-flashing earth's grand day
  In Freedom's beams!

LEAVES.

WHEN joyous Spring first clothed the trees
  How beautiful and bright
The leaves were dancing in the breeze,
  And flashing in the light!

While Summer glow'd with fiery breath
  Fresh vigour still they found,

And laugh'd away the spectre Death,
  And tinkling spurn'd the ground.

With dying glories Autumn came
  Before chill Winter's gloom,
And kindled his funereal flame
  That decks leaves for the tomb.

Now, crisp'd and brown and torn and dry,
  Before the breeze's breath
They break and fall and whirl and fly,
  The saddest types of death.

But as from leaves in dark decay
  Majestic forests rise,
We'll spring from dust in Life's great day
  Immortal for the skies.

THE HILLS.

WALK upon the Hills. The Autumn
      smoke
  Beneath curtains the vale; not only
      scenes,
But sounds are mellow'd in the haze. The corn,

Yellow and full, torn from its wither'd stalk
Without a crackling sharpness, on the ear
Soft-rustles. Half hid by elms, th' ancient mill,
Gigantic in the mist, and spectre-like
And dim, hushing its huge ponderous wheel,
Now rumbles in the vapoury distance.
Loud Industry its energy subdues,
Made gentle by the spirit of the day,
And aloft sends round sweet mingling murmurs.
The axe—no more with quick successive strokes
Piercing the ear—gives forth a lingering sound ;
The far flail muffles its thunders, beating
Heavily as that scared pheasant's doubtful wing.
The shrieking train across the rattling bridge,
Whirling with breath of smoke and eye of flame,
Swift as a rushing tempest, fills the vales
With gentle sounds as of a monster tamed.
Why from you, ye Hills, but echoes waked ?
Why on you no murmuring fields with grains
Made golden by the sun ? Say, why upon
Your breasts no orchards drop their autumn-fruits,
Or vineyards show their clusters to the day ?
Why do these hamlets gleam, these cities lift,
Lofty and bright, their spires alone from vales ?
O'er your ribb'd sides Art rears no monuments,
And Traffic wakes no hum. 'Tis yours to stand
Sublime, but desolate. 'Tis yours, ye Hills !

To wreathe your cliffs with mists that feed the
    springs,
And catch the clouds, gigantic as yourselves,
As comes their fleecy vastness from the sea
To robe your forms, and crown your tops with
    snows,
And pour enriching rivers o'er the world.
Your rocks, ye Hills! the busy cities build;
The stately shaft from you, and graceful arch,
And circling dome, and those majestic shapes
Where sacred Art immortal virtue shrines.
From you the navies vast that float the seas,
And bear their conquering thunders round the
    world.
Ye see the empires rise, ye see them fall,
While ye eternal stand.   And you, ye Hills!
Bold guardians ever rise of Liberty.
She lives amid your cliffs, she breathes your airs,
She leaps your crags, until her arm can bear
Aloft the banner of triumphant states.
Our souls with you soar to sublimity.
Great Hills! ye too Jehovah's altars stand,
Rear'd up by Him above the sordid earth
That man may kneel and worship nearer Heav'n!

PAUL PARSON.

HERE Alleghany's peaks aspire,
Now bathed in evening's crimson fire,
Now touch'd with morning's golden
    glow,
Paul Parson on his mule would go.

Long, slender, pale, and clothed in black,
Paul straddled o'er the creature's back;
Then left his inn with bow and smile,
And canter'd on a pleasant mile.

Behold him go through town and bridge,
Wind round the vale and mount the ridge,
Dashing so proudly on his way,
Like some gay knight of ancient lay!

But lo! the mule with roguish leer
Arrests this glory's bright career,
Plants down his legs, stiff as the dead,
To tumble Parson o'er his head.

Paul bawls and pulls and beats and kicks,—
He just as well might pound on bricks;
He jerks the rein, he whacks the face,
But stubbornness still keeps its place.

Now in a moment, quick as light,
Like some wild deer winged on by fright,
See, flashing, dashing, here and there,
Paul's long thin shanks sweep through the air!

From stirrups loosed, Paul's dangling legs
Bob to and fro like wooden pegs,
While thumping, bumping, on he goes,
With outstretch'd arms and upturn'd nose.

His form bent forward as he flies,
And starting from his head two eyes,
With two coat-tails outstreaming wide,
Paul fears the dust will mar his pride.

Then after five swift-glancing miles,
A quiet nestling village smiles,
Where the tired mule with quivering breast,
Stops in the street to take his rest.

Doors open fly, up windows rise,
Shop, store, and bar-room furnish eyes,
Till dark with heads the town appears,
While Gossip laughs at Parson's tears.

Back goes the mule, and back and back;
Whack Parson's whip, and whack and whack!
Till he dismounts, with weary feet,
To lead the beast along the street.

Muse, shall I sing how Parson ask'd
Help from a *woman* as he pass'd ?
How to a fence, the mule possess'd,
Leaning his weight, Paul's long limb press'd ?

As evening's shades fall on the plain
Comes through the calm the bull-frog's strain ;
As evening's star looks through the cloud
More loud the croakers and more loud.

But when o'er heav'n night's curtains roll
New courage lights our hero's soul ;
High strong resolves inflame his head
And Victory hovers round his bed.

Now as the morning tints the sky,
Paul, mounted, smiles, and says—" Good-bye ! "
But scarce his farewell reach'd his host
When stopp'd the mule, fix'd as a post.

Again he flies with whip and spur ;
Behind his heels each village cur,
Till on his path of beams the sun
One half his splendid course had run.

Ah ! wedged between two walls, crack ! crack !
A shiver'd window strews Paul's back ;
The damage too his purse must pay
Before he can go on his way.

While yet the sun with cloudless beam
Glows over Alleghany's stream
Kittaning saw Paul's image fall
On blazing street and quivering wall.

No conqueror, when his plume may wave
Where battling hosts have found a grave,
More proud than Parson when that mule,
Submissive, show'd that man will rule.

ASEL'S SOLILOQUY.

STRANGE! that to me earth's Sabbath birth e'er gave!
Sweet as the bloom hung round our fragrant wall,
Bright as young morning on the river wave,
Soft as the tones when evening shadows fall,
The bliss which o'er our Christian home had sway,
Since there the Cross, once hated, was its all;
Nor dim the light of the millennial ray
When Heav'n a thousand years streamed o'er our world in day.

War saw his sword, hung in its scabbard, rust;
No madden'd nations then were drench'd in gore

The battle-flag was long resolved to dust,
And Love with Truth and Peace ruled every
    shore;
Mankind one nation seem'd for evermore,
And earth a single temple rear'd for praise,
With Heav'n's mild glory spread a covering o'er,
While lands to answering lands their anthems
    raise
And hymn the King of all with universal lays.

My nature monstrous in that holy age;
A string, in childhood, jarring on its lyre;
Where else was bright a spot upon its page,
A rushing smoke-jet in a calm, bright fire;
A lion in my play, and in mine ire,
'Mid gentle kids disporting on the grass;
Nor brain, nor nerve, nor foot, nor limb would tire
In those mad venturous deeds which ever glass
Within the boy the tempests o'er the man to pass.

I track'd the wild beast to his quiet lair
And woke again the savage in his breast;
I shot the soaring eagle in the air
Or pierced him sitting on his mountain-nest.
Inaccessible peaks I scaled alone,
On dizzy rocks with tempests sought my rest,
Or climb'd high up, where Silence has her throne,
Or on the ocean dash'd, and felt his waves mine
    own.

A SONG IN HEAVEN TO HOME.

OH! sweet Home of my Childhood, I
    think of thee now,
  With the light of this glory so bright
    on my brow;
Since 'twas Heav'n ordain'd thee, dear place of my
    birth,
Here, here, I'll forget thee never more than on
    earth.

When my mother I see with her harp in her hand
By the throne of her King in her sweet beauty
    stand,
Then, blest Home of my Childhood, I can but recall
Her love and her face, and oh! the tear that would
    fall.

And when my noble old father, so dear and so
    grand,
In the bright circle of saints I often see stand,
Yes! thou Home of my Childhood! not in heav'n
    I'd be
Should e'er cease from my soul his fond goodness
    to me.

Oh, Home of my Childhood! when the angels do
    sing
In their rapture about the high throne of their
    King,
As I shine with the throng, as I gaze through the
    light,
There, thy soft tender image will float o'er my
    sight.

And as long as the ages eternal shall roll
Their fresh tides of glory still more bright o'er a
    soul,
Ever, Home of my Childhood, thy mem'ry will be,
As the years shall flow onward, so much dearer
    to me.

A PARLOUR PROLOGUE.

NOT in Art's temple towering to the skies,
    Where tier on tier the circling galleries
    rise;
Not 'mid the brilliance flashing o'er the stage
Where Genius paints the manners of the age;
Not where the pictured curtain rolls on high
And gives the drama's scenes to charm the eye;
Not where applauding thousands clap and yell,
Fitz-James to Mary Ann his love will tell,

Bareacres sham, and Angelina blush
When shows the footman in her dear La Plush.
Ours not the noisy crowd, the swelling dome;
We greet our friends within this smiling home.
For *snobs* we go to our ancestral land,
Nor yet deny they flourish best at hand;
Indeed 'twas thought such creatures thrived alone
Within the shadows of a monarch's throne;
But thine, my Country, thine it is to show,
Beneath thy stars and stripes they perfect grow.
They live, they die, most rich, most prized, most
    bold,
Where waves thy Flag in heav'n its proudest fold;
And in some future day, some inspired hour,
When feels our genius its immortal power,
We'll turn from royal Britain's lordly isle,
And o'er our *native* Shoddy make you smile.

NEAR MY BIRTH-PLACE.

FRAIL as that shell whose sail is o'er the
    sea
  Thence I, a tiny, throbbing, infant thing,
Forth voyaged on my immortality.
Oh, Peril stands to tear each bark's white wing,
And o'er mad billows send it shattering;
So loud the war of wind and wave before
Full sailing into bliss our souls we bring,
Where light lies golden on a waveless shore,
And the wild music of the sea resounds no more.

ISRAEL'S MARCH-WORD.

FORWARD! 'Tis Jehovah's cloud
    Leads Israel to the sea!
  Forward! Egypt fierce and proud
    Clanks chains behind the free!

Forward! Waves, thy mountain-walls,
  Shall tower along thy way!
Forward! when thy Maker calls
  'Tis madness to delay.

Forward! Where yon guiding glow
   Moves through the parted deep
Pharaoh shall lie buried low,
   In death his minions sleep.

Forward! In yon cloud and fire
   Jehovah makes His shrine.
Forward! Neither stop nor tire,
   And what is best is thine.

Forward, Israel! fear no foes!
   Thy rest is o'er the sea;
Milk there with the honey flows;
   The grape there waits for thee.

Forward! Heav'n's own fire shall die,
   And Heav'n's own manna cease;
But Jehovah thy supply,
   Thy Bread, thy Light, thy Peace.

THE HEART'S MASTER.

WHEN Morning pencils on her bright'ning
   sky
   The first faint traceries of the coming
   day
One low lone bird will trill its melody

Responsive to a solitary ray.
But as the sun floods heav'n and earth with gold
Each leaf grows tremulous with exulting strains,
That gushing, mingling, swelling high, are roll'd
Till orchestras burst out from hills, and dales, and
    plains.

And thus from some cathedral's solemn walls
A single voice will chant in melting tone,
While from a single stop the organ calls,
Thund'rous and deep, its supplicating moan.
Now hark! each tongue, each key, wakes
    music round :
Peal upon peal, on billows billows rise,
Till all the temple shakes with bursting sound
From that majestic choir which even thrills the
    skies.

In some lone vale of Heav'n an angel strays
To view its glories in soft mellow'd light:
See! o'er his harp involuntary plays
His trembling hand—his lip moves to the sight;
One murmuring strain awakes a thousand
    strings :
Lofty and full, a gathering tide soon breaks ;
Voice answers voice, to seraph seraph sings,
And in the mingling praise a universe partakes.

And thus! O Christian, is it with thy heart.
Each single chord with earthly music thrills;
Wife, parent, child, and country have their part;
When Friendship strikes her string pure rapture
 fills.
But only Christ, the Master, wakes the whole,
Can touch each key, can harmonize each tone,
And through His Cross stir love through *all*
 the soul,
To burst, Immortal King, in songs around Thy
 throne!

FOR THE BOOK OF A FRIEND.

THE ancient artist from each form and
 face
 A soft expression steals, or line of grace,
Until in one great work all beauties glow
And Heav'n's ideal breathes on earth below.
Not from the body doom'd to sad decay,
Whose wasting features death must hide from day,
But from the Mind, immortal as its sire,
Whose flame shall burn when brilliant suns expire,
May choicest gifts to thy loved page impart
A lustre brighter than the painter's art!

Best Friend, let Reason, smiling from her throne,
With gracious sceptre claim thy work her own!
Here Memory all her varied treasures bring,
And glittering Fancy wave her rainbow wing!
Then come, Religion, daughter of the skies,
Light on thy brow and Love within thine eyes,
Thy garland weave, thou best-beloved of Art,
And paint the virtues of a Christian heart!

THE ALL-MAKER.

WHAT is the universe but His sole will
    Who from Himself did first create the all,
And with His own great Omnipresence fill
The unseen atom and the peopled ball,
And without Whom nor leaf nor world may fall?
He of His works is force, and law, and soul,
And His invisible breath alone can call
The spirit out from naught, or worlds forth roll,
And round Himself, the centre, make revolve the whole.

Each life is from His Life, and all the bloom
Which robes the earth with the bright-budding spring
In glory bursting from the winter's tomb

Is but Himself, when He would beauty fling
From His o'erflowing fullness, and would bring
Bliss from Himself, unmarr'd, except by sin.
Himself removed, and of His works each thing
Of sense is naught, while spirits feel within
The worm and fire from which none but Himself
  can win.

INVOCATION.

WHEN in the east bright purpling morn
  Proclaims another day is born,
  And o'er some hill the kingly sun
Rides forth his radiant race to run,
The blushing moon, the star retires
To hide from view their modest fires.
But though invisible their ray
Within the brighter blaze of day,
They shine, they roll, nor pause nor rest,
With living millions on each breast.
Thus Fancy, Reason, Art, engage
To pour your splendours o'er my page,
And yet, as stars, when bursts the light,
Withdraw their glittering globes from sight,
So may your radiance fade away
Before Religion's brighter day!

THE RAINBOW.

MYSTERIOUS Bow! born from the
    rain and light,
How silently thine arch is flung o'er
    heav'n!
What Power invisible arrests his beams
Bright flashing from the sun, their hues untwists,
And curves them o'er our world in majesty?
Round, matchless Form! do spirits in thee dwell,
And bend thee down the sky, and weave thy
    charms,
And run along thy glittering sides, and smile
From thee o'er man rejoicing in thy peace?
Who lifts into the air these tints of earth,
The soft green of leaves, the violet's hue,
The gold of fruits, the crimson of the rose,
And all the varied garniture of seasons?
Twas God thy grace conceived! He breathes thy
    hues;
He hangs thee in the cloud, His pledge of peace;
He bends thee round across the lonely sea
In which thy glory curves to tinge its waves.
O'er boundless plains thy circling colours smile,
Or soar aloft to span the gloom of woods,

While towering high into thy gorgeous tints
The spires of cities float.   Grandly o'er vales,
Pillar'd on mountain-tops, great Bow of Light,
Majestically high thy glory stands,
Bright type of Love, uniting Earth and Heav'n!

A VISION OF SOLYMA.

SWEET on the air was breathing fragrant
   June,
  And tempting to her bloom the murmuring bee,
When, pass'd the blazing splendours of the noon,
Upon the grass I slept beneath a tree,
Whose leaves arch'd o'er, a whispering canopy.
Proud as a queen waved near my head a rose,
And blossoms round my dreamy eyes could see;
High in the heav'ns a summer sun still glows,
And sailing o'er his face no cloud its shadow
   throws.

I dream'd earth's storms were hush'd, nor roar'd
   one sea;
Serene bent down the blue eternal skies:

From pain and death our world forever free
Show'd smiles more sweet than those of Paradise.
Music the ear, all beauty thrill'd mine eyes:
Perfection o'er the scene doth glory throw:
No tear-drop glistens, and no lip breathes sighs,
While in each breast Love whispers soft and low,
And Heav'n comes down to earth where joy will ever grow.

High on a central hill a City shone
Bathed in a glory of celestial light:
Not dull with tarnish'd time-decaying stone:
Its gems and gold were flashing on my sight,
In beams from One whose face dispell'd the night.
O'er the new earth it shone the pride and queen,
More dazzling than the sun noon-crown'd with light,
So bright, that by mere mortal vision seen,
'Twould blind and burn the eye with its resplendent sheen.

Hast thou look'd on the Alps while yet the Spring
Left on their sides the pure long-lingering snow,

And down some mountain gorge the sun did fling
In floods the splendours of his parting glow,
Till steeps and peaks to walls and turrets grow?
A glittering city floating seem'd in air,
By angels built, whose forms still come and go:
One passing cloud soon spoil'd the pageant rare,
But left in thee the types which do last things declare.

Yes! thus on earth, in vision veil'd and dim,
Could musing men 'mid Alpine heights behold,
Oh Solyma! a dazzling vision swim
Of thy gem-flashing walls and streets of gold.
By them remember'd when thy charms unfold.
But oh! how poor at eve that mountain-sight,
When thy true glories are to eyes unroll'd,
Where Beauty's self doth live to make thee bright,
And pour upon thee still her everlasting light!

There is in man a deep earth cannot fill:
A throb in eyes for charms they may ne'er see,
An ache in ears for strains that never thrill,
In hearts a cry for something yet to be—
Some bliss supreme, fix'd as eternity.

Time mocks the dream it never can destroy;
Men shadows chase fast as the shadows flee,
Yet flying tell of bliss without alloy
In *some* immortal state where but to live is joy.

Oft had I felt humanity's great pain—
The void that craves in this our mortal lot:
To fill it grasp'd, and ever grasp'd in vain,
And found I wish'd a boon which earth had not,
And saw on all her good a blackening blot.
But, oh! when Solyma burst on mine eyes,
There, there I knew the life without a spot:
There, there would lift the veil with glad surprise,
And on existence show the bloom that never dies!

And now soft music stole out on mine ear
Like some old prelude to an evening hymn:
Then burst a vision beautiful e'en here,
Where harmony must breathe in face and limb,
Conforming always to some mould of Him
In Whom, concentred, manhood finds its all,
And from Whom rays out glory to the rim
Of His Creation, and will robing fall
A light on all fair things which we may lovely call.

Oh Florence! raptured, I have charm'd mine eye
With that sweet marble, shedding fame o'er thee,
Which caught in Greece of many an age the sigh,
Till *one* could fix its immortality
And cut in stone a dream where all agree
A spark alone flash'd down from Attic skies
Could kindle into light a shape so free
From mortal blot, and which o'er time will rise,
Expressing mankind's thought that unembodied dies.

City of Art! glass'd bright in Arno's tide,
In thee no form like that I saw may shine,
O'er which eternal beauty can preside,
Live in each part and breathe in every line,
And by years undimm'd th' Artist prove divine.
Upturn'd and beaming still I see the face
Which seem'd of bliss itself a holy sign,
While limb and feature soften'd o'er with grace,
And flow'd a melody beseeming well the place.

On earth there was in hearts a sigh,
  And the dull throb of pain:
The tear-drop trembled in the eye,
  Then fell, to fall again.

Oh! Change o'er all a shadow threw,
   His brother Death was there,
And e'en the sparkle of the dew
   Soon vanish'd into air.

Wild phantoms o'er the mind would rush,
   With pain the body thrill,
And ere the brimming cup could blush
   The tempting wine would spill.

The love that on the warm lip press'd
   To leave its tender kiss,
Would soon lean o'er a cold, cold breast,
   And find a woe for bliss.

But here, on all things is the bloom
   Which lives without decay,
And He who brought us from the tomb
   Makes our immortal day.
       Hallelujah!

Sometimes, when Evening sets her golden star
Bright in the trembling bosom of the lake,
From a dim mountain cliff, heard high and far,
A musing shepherd's song will softly break
And sleeping echoes in the rocks awake;
Lip answers lip, and sound replies to sound,

And as new breasts new inspirations take,
That twilight music swells and spreads around,
Until from peak to peak the melodies rebound.

And thus the strain that floated from that hill,
Borne distant on the calm, celestial air,
A single saint enraptured with its thrill,
And then a flame of glory kindles there,
Till mingling millions in the joy do share.
Hark! Hallelujah rings from height to height!
To seraphs, seraphs loud the word declare!
Far burst the sounds through all the worlds of light,
And that one song with praise a universe makes bright.

Waked by my bliss, my dream was gone—how soon!
And where the noon had beam'd upon mine eye
I saw a pale star near the infant moon
Whose silver circle pencill'd o'er the sky,
While glittering round the pole the Wain wheel'd high.
A thundering cloud made earth more drear and dim,
And for each joy before I breathed a sigh;
Yet from the music-burst of that bright sphere
One low and lingering note lives murmuring in mine ear.

THE USEFUL AND THE BEAUTIFUL.

    'TIS only when rough roots below
      Unsightly masses tangled throw
        Both deep and wide,
  Majestically the tree can rise
  Which time and storm to age defies,
    In stately pride.

  Unpolish'd rocks, from hills convey'd,
  Deep in the solid earth are laid
    By careful hands,
  Before the house where art would reign
  Lifts high its beauty from the plain
    And stately stands.

  If forms which please, profuse and bright,
  Their brilliant colours flash to sight
    And charm the view,
  Yet, firm as their Almighty Cause,
  Has Reason all things bound in laws
    As numbers true.

  Learn, while the Beautiful may smile
  From flower to star, and care beguile,

Life's charm and grace,
The Useful yet beneath must lie
All loveliness of earth and sky,
Creation's base.

WRITTEN FOR A LADY, TO BE GIVEN WITH HER PHOTOGRAPH.

THE costly jewel and the clasp of gold
Oft glitter on the gift when love is cold.
I ask not here the aid of brilliant art
To gild the priceless friendship of the heart.
Wilt thou accept myself, and her survey,
Well known when youth danced bright along our way?
Now as life smiles amid our clouds and tears,
The woman seals the love of girlhood's years.
When fades this image painted by the sun,
When shadows flee, when substance is begun,
May we together rise from dust and night,
Where Friendship brightens in eternal light!

ON A BIRTHDAY.

MEMORY, Love, recalls the day
    When morning shade and sunlight lay
        Upon the grass;
The heav'ns look'd down in cloudless blue,
The rose breathed fragrance from its dew,
And Earth smiled in her loveliest hue,
        To see thee pass.

Thy cheek was bloom, thine eye was light,
And love and hope and beauty bright
        Were in thy face;
As Memory sees thee through the years,
Untouch'd by time, undimm'd by tears,
No flow'r when opening spring appears
        Unfolds such grace.

Since, on life's path, the cloud and storm
Have sometimes darken'd round thy form
        And swept thy sky;
Yet trial's years in heart and brow
Have made thee fairer to me now
Than when in youth thy marriage vow
        Brighten'd mine eye.

If, blushing round some elder rose,
The sweet buds burst, the gay flow'r glows,
    Beneath green trees;
But statelier its maternal pride
To see such beauty at its side,
And know that mingled perfumes glide
    Out on the breeze.

LIFE.

HOW awful Life! scarce one bright insect-thing,
    Warm'd by a sunbeam to a moment's flight,
Can drop amid its summer fluttering
And change its little day for sudden night,
But sends a shudder o'er my wondering sight.
Yet not each world alone; each atom, teems
With that which moves and feels; yon very light,
Binding the universe around with beams,
Hides life's mysteries where it, dancing, joys and gleams.

Oh! what then Mind, with impulse, passion, thought—
That which can love and hate and fear and will—

A quickening spirit into being brought,
Now pierced with pain, now keen with pleasure's thrill,
A something time nor space nor worlds can fill,
Once struck, a spark for evermore to blaze—
May be flash forth immortal millions, till
Souls thick as stars shall be to curse or praise
In lives that *must* go on through everlasting days!

THE DEITY.

 GOD, Thy temple is the Universe!
Thy Presence fills its All, and, till It was,
Eternal solitude enshrined Thy Majesty!
Yes! Being's chain begins and ends in Thee—
From and by and for whom is existence.
In the wild mystic circuits of their change,
Impell'd by Thee, the elements combine.
Light shines Thy brightness circled in vast suns,
Diffusing thence Thy beams to glimmering worlds.
Th' electric essence bursting from the clouds
In thunder-bolts or tamed to flash man's thought,
A universal force, the subtle link
Of flesh and soul, Thine own volition darts.
Form, Number, Law, are what but Thee express'd,

And Beauty, Grandeur, and Sublimity?
Thy colours paint the world! Thy hand bends
 round
The glittering rainbow's arch! Majestic stands
 in Thee
The dome of Heav'n! Thy breath the breeze
That lifts the flower, and curls the wave, and steals
O'er murmuring leaves to cool the fever'd brow.
The Seasons pass Thy visible glory!
Storms, billows, earthquakes, motions of Thy will,
And souls, immortal sparks struck out from Thee!
Thy Power the bond, Thy Intellect the guide,
Thy Presence the circumference of all!

SOLICITUDE.

I TREMBLE, love, when in my breast
   I see thine image lie;
To me bright beauty, which no art
Could from the dreams of genius start
   In forms to please the eye.

  The morning heav'ns which blush and glow
    Reflected in the stream
  But on its *surface* splendours throw,
  Nor waters tinge that glide below,
    Unconscious of a beam.

Thy love through *all* my being reigns,
    As when the painter's dye
Each canvas-thread pervades and stains
And if a fragment but remains
    Its colours you descry.

I start to hear my heart-strings break—
    Each life-hope rent away;
The ruin fancy death could make,
The weary blank, the dull cold ache,
    The midnight where smiled day.

Then Faith takes wing,—beyond the tomb,
    In God's eternal sky,
Our love shall live where shades no gloom,
And Christ to all imparts the bloom
    Of Immortality.

REGRET.

 A TEARFUL mourner kneels beside a grave
    Along whose green is mingling autumn's gold,
While through the hazy mists mute branches wave
    And crimson leaves a dying year unfold.

REGRET.

Back from the mystic past what mem'ries teem!
   A bride's bright beauty smiling rises now;
In evening's hush beside the moonlit stream
   He hears again the silver-whisper'd vow.

The white-robed priest, the brilliant festal throng,
   The rainbow glory Hope o'er youth did throw,
The wedded years, like golden light and song,
   Gild e'en the tomb with momentary glow.

But why that cloud as shakes yon kneeling form?
   Why does a tear-drop burn the throbbing eye?
Thus from the hills will sweep the midnight storm
   To veil the summer-moon and tranquil sky.

Does a wife's death-scene make such anguish start?—
   The last seen smile, the agonized farewell,
The life-ties tearing from an aching heart—
   That pang of lonely grief we may not tell?

Ah no! 'tis but a *word* spreads o'er this gloom
   Whose tone once thrill'd the ear that sleeps with pain,
And now comes thundering from the solemn tomb,
   By memory waked, 'till heard through years again·

Oh! when we drop upon the grave a tear
   And Love rolls back the curtains of the past,
May all its scenes unstain'd and bright appear,
   Nor dark Regret with clouds the heart o'ercast!

ABRAHAM LINCOLN.

AJESTIC on a mountain height
    And crown'd by morn's first glow,
A pine for ages flash'd the light
    Far down the vales below.

And often would bright sunbeams play
    Around that monarch-form,
When black beneath the night-mists lay
    Or roar'd the darkening storm.

'Tis evening. Hark! Quick murderous blows!
    A crash! that tall pine died!
Where tempests vain in wrath arose
    An *axe* pierced through its side.

And towering, rooted in the right,
    Our Martyr in our state
First caught the beams of Freedom's light,
    First caught the storms of hate.

And did he fall by one mean hand
    Who had wild millions braved?
Earth's tyrants know his *work* shall stand
    And Liberty be saved!

As from the mountain-pine's decay
A loftier tree may rise,
That Martyr higher lifts in day
.The cause for which he dies.

BIRDS AT MORN.

WAKED from my dreams I smiled, and saw the day
As burst the young sun from his golden shroud,
And slanted from his jocund face a ray,
Which, tinting morning on her crimson cloud,
Inspired the tuneful birds to warble loud,
As if the King of Heav'n, brimm'd o'er with joy,
Did flash his beams to pipe within that crowd,
And thus benign the feathery throats employ
To one glad chorus give without earth's sad alloy.

ABOVE.

HOW the winds are ever blowing,
Which the flying clouds compel!
How the streams are ever flowing
The majestic seas to swell!

How the golden mists, ascending
  To the sun from ocean's face,
Drop the rain by Heav'n's intending,
  Rills and rivers to replace !

Day and night o'er earth are throwing
  Both their brightness and their gloom,
While Death, chasing Life, is mowing
  Ceaseless harvests for the tomb.

Seasons pass, and Time advancing
  Makes the empires rise and fall,
Till man sees, wherever glancing,
  Desolations which appal.

But *above* are always glowing
  Mystic worlds serenely bright,
With no tempests madly blowing,
  With no shadows of the night.

O'er earth's changes they are sweeping
  In serenity sublime,
Held by Him within whose keeping
  Are Eternity and Time.

Even could their spheres, decaying,
  Be hurl'd back into night,
Soul, believing and obeying,
  Thy Eternity is light.

THE *CLOUDS.

OW beautiful the Clouds! From night
    distill'd,
  Their stealthy mists creep low along the
    fields,
Hang o'er the streams, or climbing round the hills
Spread an expanse illimitably white,
With trees like islands lifting through their green,
Touch'd by the gold and crimson of the morn.
Or gathering from the sky-encircled sea,
Clouds hide its face and run along its shores,
Then, rising grandly with the kingly sun,
Float o'er the heav'ns. And infinite their forms!
Diffused and grey and dim, now a mere breath,
They scarce will stain the blue whose dome roofs
    round,
Sublime and vast, our world, while soon they troop
Along the sky like full-fleeced flocks of spring.
Clouds, touch'd as by some hand invisible,
Will take artistic shapes, and silent form
A beautiful mosaic of the heav'ns;
First leaden, dull, then tinged with bronze and gold,
Or fringed with red volcanic lines of flame.

The Rain-Clouds with their vapours fill the air,
Moist, uniform, and low, while Nimbus high,
Distent with casual showers, floats by himself,
Oft o'er the zenith hung. Storm-Clouds, how wild!
By tempests borne behold them sweep near earth,
Straggling and thin below, ashen above,
And higher still a midnight black, frowning,
And terrible—mass piled on dark'ning mass—
Not torn and shatter'd by the driving winds,
But in huge solid columns towering far,
They rush on demon-wing across the sky
With solemn earnestness that seems
Intent to reach the limits of the world.
How calm and white the noble Cumulus!
Great King of Clouds, silent and grand and high,
His throne push'd forth, grows vast as Heav'n
    itself—
Blanc lifted into air—rather all Alps—
Peak upon snowy peak, and ridge on ridge,
With ever-changing tops, involved and round,
That circle with a boiling whirlpool's force,
By the quick lightnings cross'd, while from their
    deep
Retiring vales growl low the summer thunders.
Gorgeous the pomp of clouds that waits the sun!
Behold his heralds flaming o'er the east!
A fringe! a belt! fold burnishing o'er fold!

Y

What hues! what forms! varieties of glory!
Purple and gold, and mountains bright of flame!
Heav'n's resplendent wealth pour'd out on the
  mists,
That curl, and glow, and burn as lifts the sun,
'Mid floods of rays, his head above the world
In silent, dazzling, kingly majesty!
The evening's tints how rich and delicate!
Those crimson stains, those vistas in the sky
That fade into infinity, with hues
Serene and exquisite! Those silver lines!
Those isles of light! Those palaces of gold
Where angels watch, and wave their glittering
  wings!
Glory so bright, yet oft by man unseen,
  Streaming o'er Heav'n effulgence like God's
  throne!
Nor, ye Clouds, are ye but painted splendours
Born to please the eye! Rains do form in you
To feed the world! Keep in the skies your drops,
And flowers fall from their stems, and forests
  die,
And harvests fail, and cease the murmuring
  streams!
Nay! seas would vanish in the burning suns,
And, void of you, our earth would roll a tomb.
Ye bright, fantastic shapes that deck the skies,

Our hope and life, floating from land and sea
Aloft o'er Heav'n, rise, Clouds, in beauty rise,
Wafting like fragrance from the censer's gold,
Glowing and pure, the grateful love of Earth!

BOABDIL'S LAMENT ON THE HILL OF TEARS.

GRANADA! thy king weeps in sight of thy walls;
His crown on his foe, a lone exile he stands;
And his heart left behind in Alhambra's halls
He goes for his grave to far infidel lands.

In Mem'ry how fair groves, fountains, and bowers,
The silver of moonlight o'er Alhambra's art!
A lute's note of love steals aloft to those towers
As mine once arose to the maid of my heart.

Hark! festival music swells high on the air
Gay forms of dancers float again o'er my sight!
I seem on my throne 'mid the brave and the fair,
As Alhambra's glories stream wide through the night.

In palace and street turban'd heads I behold !
My steed paws the street and my banner's unfurl'd !
Bright gleam from yon minarets crescents of gold !
Bride of Heav'n, Granada smiles Queen of the world !

'Tis Fancy's false dream, and thy glory is gloom !
By cannon I see thy tall battlements torn !
No rose on thy wall ! on the orange no bloom !
Thy knights are in chains, and an exile I mourn.

Yes ! Infidel swords in thy streets flash their flames,
And Infidel songs e'en now burst from thy halls !
The Infidel priest thine own Prophet defames !
The Infidel cross gleams o'er Alhambra's walls !

Be done Allah's will ! This my star did foretell,
That rose o'er a throne but to set in a grave ;
The Moor's empire is o'er ! Granada, farewell !
Thy king drops a tear for thy fair, good, and brave !

AYXA'S REBUKE FOR BOABDIL'S LAMENT.

LAMENTS for the coward! for frail woman be tears!
Let the weak breasts of lovers heave their sighs to their fears!
But the eye of the warrior with lightnings should flame,
And the lip of the warrior should battle proclaim.

Had my purple scarf broken o'er Alhambra's stones,
And thy proud father stifled the breath of thy moans;
Had the Arabic steed whose hoof thunder'd through night
Hurl'd thee down from his neck o'er the precipice height;

Had the stern Hassan's courage but flash'd from thine eye;
Thy banner had Zagal wide unfurl'd to the sky;

Had chivalrous Musa worn thy crest and thy
    crown,
And thy steel gleam'd in death where thy gold
    was paid down ;

Had the zeal of the Christian burn'd hot in thy soul
When we saw o'er our hills his curs'd Cross first
    unroll ;
Had thy mother's own heart in thy bosom beat
    warm,
Spurning Infidel leagues, daring battle's wild
    storm ;

Then, Granada, thy towers would have stood on
    the earth ;
There no Infidel guard, there no Infidel mirth ;
And on Alhambra now no Cross would be seen,
Where the Crescent in glory flash'd for ages its
    sheen.

Oh Boabdil ! he who would rule must be brave,
And if reft of a throne must choose next a grave.
'Twas not Fate by thy star sank Granada in
    gloom:
But thy weak, coward heart is thine empire's sad
    tomb.

MADRIGAL.

OPEN, Love, thy lattice wide!
   Let the moonbeam pass!
See it through the branches glide!
   See it on the grass!

Open, Love, thy lattice now!
   Let the breeze come through!
Let it play around thy brow,
   And thy bosom woo!

Open, Love, the lattice, while
   I gaze up on thee!
Let yon star-beam kiss a smile
   From thy lip to me!

Love, thy lattice wide, wide fling!
   Be like yon bright sky!
While the sea is murmuring
   It bends lovingly.

SERENADE.

SLEEP, Love, with smiling dreams!
    Bright o'er thy bed
    Some rosy head!
Light-wing'd the boy-god gleams.
    Sleep, Love!

Sleep, till his arrow flies.
    Twang, twang, the dart
    Goes to thy heart;
He laughing mounts the skies.
    Sleep, Love!

Wake, Love, and see the moon!
    Beam like yon star,
    But not afar,
And fling a kiss down soon!
    Wake, Love!

ART AND NATURE.

THE picture view! what wild sublimity!
    Omnipotence has waked and hurl'd the
        storm,
Tossing the deep to tumult. Round that tower

Rising defiant on its ocean-rock,
Dashes the maniac wave, whose flying spray,
Hung high in air, before the tempest streams,
While sea-birds circle on exultant wing,
Silent and calm, above the foam and roar
Of battling elements. A mystic spell
Enchains as we admire, O Man, thy skill.
But draw near the canvas. Th' illusion fades,
And rough, unseemly colours shock the eye
Where genius breath'd to waken ecstasy.
And *this* is Art !   Ye forms of ancient Greece,
That in her temples hung to kindle ages,
And ye which smile along Italia's walls,
Or charm 'neath colder suns—Immortal Works,
Yet were and are ye rough when seen so near ?
Not Nature thus ! Her worlds behold on worlds,
Systems round systems rolling ever on
To fill a universe with light and life,
And then draw close and scan her smallest parts.
The glittering drop, the blushing peach's down,
The yellow dust that loads the murmuring bee,
A feather's tint, an insect's golden wing,
All, all, the far, the near, are exquisite.

MY ROSE.

MY noble Rose, crown'd Queen of flowers,
    What makes thy lovely hues?
  Is it the drops of summer showers?
    Is it the morning dews?

How can that black and scentless earth
    Which round thy roots is seen
Give this delicious fragrance birth
    And soften in thy green?

Or do these whispers of the air
    Waving thy graceful stem
A beauty give which kings despair
    To purchase in a gem?

May be, from golden realms of light
    Some dancing sunbeam weaves
This bloom of glory, rich and bright,
    That lingers in thy leaves.

Or with the blushes of the morn
    From heav'n an angel flies,
And spreads these colours which adorn,
    More splendid than his skies.

MY ROSE.

Can a celestial spirit hide
   Now in thy circling bloom,
And lift thy stem in stately pride
   And shed thy sweet perfume?

Oh what, my Rose! with mystic power
   Forever thus commands
To thee, a perishable flower,
   Our eyes and hearts and hands?

The eternal thought of God thou art,
   His beauty to enshrine:
The charm that binds thee to each heart
   Resistless, is divine.

THE REAL AND THE IDEAL.

CAN, oh Spirit! thine Ideal
   Be obscured by mists of earth,
While this dull, exacting Real
   Stifles a celestial birth?

Why thrill senses form'd for pleasure
   With this agony of pain?
Why do powers without a measure
   Never here their sphere attain?

Why are plans forever failing
   In this selfishness of strife?
Why are hearts forever wailing,
   Crush'd beneath the load of life?

Oh! must we, to Heav'n aspiring,
   By earth's cares and duties bound,
Sink till, with the struggle tiring,
   Grovelling we love the ground?

Spirit, trust! since all is tending
   To thy work and growth above,
Where thy powers will live, ascending
   In eternal truth and love.

Fix'd in Heav'n our grand Ideal,
   Bright beyond the clouds of time,
Then, pursued on earth the Real,
   Life, made true, becomes sublime.

THE END.

CHISWICK PRESS:—PRINTED BY WHITTINGHAM AND WILKINS,
TOOKS COURT, CHANCERY LANE.

www.ingramcontent.com/pod-product-compliance
Lightning Source LLC
Chambersburg PA
CBHW031858220426
43663CB00006B/677